REFUGEE MEMOIRS

by Tom Zed (aka Tomek Ziolkowski, aka Tomasz)

For my parents, for affording me a truly perfect childhood and upbringing, despite the tough Communist rule and Cold War era. And that my dad, having been away at sea, as a ship's officer for much of the time, leaving Mum in charge of everything, never had any negative impact on me, and only makes my memories sweeter, for his returns home ...

It never occurred to me to this day (my older sister reminded me about this 'dysfunctionality' of our childhood only recently), that it was strange, not having both – Mum and Dad there all the time. But for me, a young boy, fascinated with his father's ships when visiting on board and how it was like Christmas every time he came back home, showering us with exotic gifts;

it more than compensated for the frequent separation.

What a pain I would have caused you, leaving for good, with a one-way ticket, as a teen.

Glad time healed us and that we met again, several times, in my new life incarnations, years later.

With love, Tomek.

CONTENTS:

FOREWORD:

The author of *Refugee Memoirs* took on to emigrate out of the comfort of his family home and native country, Poland, as a teenager, not knowing perhaps, the full, life-changing implications laying ahead.

Adventure and the unknown were the real drivers, under the mask of a 'political refugee', as was the requirement to qualify for the status and the protection, under the Geneva Refugee Convention in 'The West'. There were tens of thousands of refugees in the camps of Vienna, Austria and elsewhere, like in West Germany, Sweden and Britain at the time, about a year or so before the Berlin Wall fell.

The transition from a relatively wealthy lifestyle to the barren *lager* (Traiskirchen and Götzendorf, where the old army barracks were made available to accommodate the masses) and queuing for meals supplied was intimidating, humbling and sobering, especially for a young, city teen.

This book is a personal take on the complexities of emigrating, immigration and a person's uprooting to another place, and more importantly, another culture. Today's globalised, almost borderless world makes it relevant, for millions of people choosing, some freely, to leave their homeland and live in another country.

Some three and a half decades later, the world is full of refugees: 69 million, to be exact, in 2018 (https://www.cbsnews.com/news/world-refugee-day-2018-almost-69-million-refugees-fled-war-violence-persecution/). Except this time, most asylum seekers are displaced by war, violence and persecution. It is unimaginable, what and where awaits their future, as governments juggle the intake quota and shy away, under the negative domestic media and public pressure to stop accepting in big numbers; citing economic, political, employment, accommodation, etc. reasons, and religious problems.

The cultural implications looming beyond the 'Welcome to Xxxxx' sign, wherever you may arrive, compounding months, years, decades later, manifested by the feeling of social misfitting, remoteness and indifference in society, grow over time and never seem to get much better. Or do they ...?

The lucky ones who get accepted into a country have only two ways in which to choose to assimilate: generally, either by focusing to seek and to stick to their own kind, without much interracial mingling in their new homeland, or taking the plunge and 'When in "Rome", do as the Romans do' ... fully adapting, mixing-in, becoming local as soon as possible, often at the cost of their identity and certainly their original culture (including the mother-tongue).

Embracing the latter, this is the author's own reflection of both – the success and the failure to make it work, away from the homeland.

I.   EUROPE, AFRICA AND BACK TO POLAND

Life was good for us, in the 1970s, as a family. We were 'well off', especially compared with most of the population oppressed behind the 'Iron Curtain' under the dictatorship of Soviet Communism in the Eastern Block.

We had a nice, big apartment (later a house/villa out of town), a new car, a new caravan, did road trips around Europe (besides the restrictions). I had a brand new JAWA Sport two-stroke motorbike; we even had a home phone! This is no bragging, but an admission that life wasn't bad at all for me, for as long as I can remember, from kindergarten, where I first started learning English, through primary school and college, including Marlboro/Camel cigarette smoking, vodka/scotch/gin drinking, Pink Floyd, Black Sabbath, and Deep Purple headbanging. Whoever said life was dull and boring under the Communist system in the Eastern Block ... we had a ball!

My apprenticeship on board my dad's cargo vessel on a voyage along the West Coast of Africa changed me, in my transition to a young adult, early in the piece. I was only a young teenager, when my father offered me the opportunity to accompany him and his crew on a 120-day sea voyage, on a 10,000 DWT vessel from the Baltic Sea, across the Kiel Canal, the

Bay of Biscay and about a dozen port calls along the West Coast of Africa; from Las Palmas (getting the supplies for the 25 or so crew) and onto Senegal, Sierra Leone, Liberia, Ivory Coast, Ghana, Togo, Benin, Nigeria, Cameroon, Gabon, Congo and Angola (and return to Poland the same way).

I would like to highlight the fact that this was in the depths of the oppressive Communist travel (and all other personal/political) restrictions, and I was left to make all my passport, visa, quarantine/health-immunisation, school-leave arrangements, while sponsored by my parents, to organise ALL myself. Independence, perseverance, red-tape-navigation and bribery lessons in fast-forward mode!

Passing the green pastures along the Kiel Canal, in the French port of Rouen, via Le Havre, in the mouth of the river Seine, provided an opportunity for the crew to do a bus tour into Paris, a couple of hours drive away. I have some great memories of the French capital, walking some of the most famous tourist attractions in the world, son and father. We took a lot of photos, as you do, including the fireworks display on the banks of the river near the centre of Paris, since it was Bastille Day celebrations. Next day, back in the ship's cabin, failing to rewind the film in the old camera, I opened it and exposed the film, ruining all of our images of the most special memories in Paris! As a little consolation to this, I was to be back in Paris sometime later, driving back to Poland, proceeding my final exit from the motherland later on.

Las Palmas, the capital of Gran Canaria, one of Spain's Canary Islands in the Atlantic Ocean, is the last stop for any vessels heading south, past Gibraltar, towards the West Coast of the African continent. That's where you shop and get supplies: fresh water, fuel, food, medicines, etc. The crew all enjoy their shore leave there, with many cheap entertainment and sex options available. Exotica, at its best! The beaches are beautiful and most crowded, making it difficult to get through to the waves, without stepping onto someone's mat, towel or limb. Oh, and it is topless for all.

As exotic as the destinations were, all of the ports along the African coast at the time were getting, or were about to get, their independence from their colonisers (i.e. Britain, Holland, France, etc.). This certainly added to the security concerns and to my adventure. I will never forget when I first smelt the sweet, fruity, humid African air when docking in Dakar (Senegal).

The indigenous traders boarding our vessel in every port would buy our European (cheap) homewares, business shoes/clothes, toiletries, simple electronic equipment, alcohol, cigarettes, chocolate, etc.; smuggled out of Poland in bulk quantities, under the term 'contraband'. This was how the crew made their real money in the merchant navy. The bartering, haggling and theatrical expressions made by the locals during our transactions taught me a lot! (I try not to pay 'retail' for anything to this day, and in the many years since my African trading experience, I have offended many a shopkeeper in developed countries, trying to haggle while buying a loaf of bread, a can of soda, or a carton of milk in a suburban shop.) Also, it made me a tough (big-ticket) buyer later in my adult life and business dealings, which was useful, although it never made me any friends. It was cringeworthy, at times, and eventually I learned to pay what is deserved by the merchant.

We had a small moped on the ship, used by the crew to get about while ashore. During one of our port calls in West Africa, without seeking my dad's permission, I disembarked and rode into the green hills, way out of town. The local kids friendly-waved to me; a white-blonde boy, with straight long hair, shining like a star (or a proverbial white elephant), while I zoomed passed their humble villages. When I got over the hills in the thick, tropical forest along the narrow, windy road; I came across a checkpoint manned by three men, wearing non-descriptive/unmarked camouflage uniforms and Kalashnikov assault rifles, in ready. I had no ID; nothing on me, but a tee, shorts and sandals.

My English was better than theirs, so with a fair degree of flamboyance, I basically fast-talked my way out of the interrogation and while still talking, turned around and blasted off in the direction I'd just come from, without looking back. No pursuit (or shots) followed and I made it back to the ship, scared for my life but unharmed. The mind boggles 'what if' in such a remote, unknown location. To this day, I have never told my father about this escapade, which could have ended tragically and mysteriously for me, all at the same time.

Our ship's agent in Abidjan, the Ivory Coast capital, took my dad and me for a car drive and a walk downtown. Skyscrapers, flash offices, Rolex, Pierre Cardin and other fancy shops, just like in Europe, but with the reminders of the Third World poverty lurking just around every corner; with beggars and the homeless, living rough on the streets, in makeshift shelters made out of cardboard boxes and pieces of broken tin and sheets of plastic. Among all this, we even went into a luxury bar (nightclub later in the evenings) with dark, mood lighting and a striptease stage in the shape of the African Continent. Three cocktails cost us a small fortune, even by European standards! Ah ... Africa!

Port stays for a cargo ship back in the days, especially in Africa, where the labour-force was not very swift or efficient, lasted several days, even without any unusual delays, which was heaven for any tourist. There were three others on board; most cargo ships had guest cabins and the shipping lines were keen on this business revenue. I was my dad's guest/son and happily we shared his cabin, not to mention my return passage fare was at staff/family rates.

Even if there were no significant tourist attractions (after seeing the ultra-exotic local markets with produce; arts and crafts; and jewellery made on the spot, with indigenous goldsmiths and their homemade gas-flame blowtorches, producing the most beautiful and cheap masterpieces ... yes, we had lots of it, since my dad worked the West African coast for over a decade), every port city had a luxury pool-bar oasis (yes, 'White Guests Only'. This was still in the depths of apartheid, while Nelson Mandela was imprisoned in a dark cell). These were fenced/gated properties, with security and impeccable service provided by the local hospitality personnel. I loved splashing in the crystal-clear freshwater pools, getting cold beers brought to my lounger. It never occurred to me how much disparity, social injustice and discrimination there was, but now I cringe that I was such an ignorant young customer. Warnings were often given to us by the expats who lived there, not to wear any expensive items, for the risk of having an arm chopped off with a machete, by some motorcycle gang on the lookout for unsuspecting, white targets with

anything of value attached to their bodies. Ah ...
Africa!

II.   THE TASTE OF WESTERN 'FREEDOM' AND 'DEMOCRACY'

On the way home from Africa, I knew it would
be difficult to adjust back. Squeezing through
the narrow Kiel Canal, the German fields and
cows grazing so close to our slowly passing ship
were a stark reminder of how close we were to
terra firma ... and the end of my voyage.

On my return home to Poland, I was a celebrity
back in school, having to report on my
experiences, under the strict teachers'
supervision, making sure I did not break any
propaganda taboos of the regime. Showing the
voyage map, telling stories, sporting a tan, I was
admired, yet felt distant from my peers. 'They'
at school, even forbade me wearing the Swiss

watch my dad gave me because it was not 'the norm'. Understandably, I guess.

It wasn't long before my parents realised I was already a 'foreign misfit' in Poland, even on my own turf. Utilising my dad's shipping contacts abroad, I took off again, this time to France, where there was a stevedoring job and accommodation made available for me and my older cousin, on the West Coast, near La Rochelle. The fast train from Paris, collected by the man who would be our host and employer over the following three to four months. We were set!

Work was hard, labouring on the wharf and the vessels alongside, but compensated with good pay, opulent accommodation and food at our boss's house – we loved it, making ourselves feel at home.

In the heat of the French summer days, the job was to bag the bulk (loose) stockfeed into 25 and 50 kg bags, carrying the bags on one's shoulder and palletising to a height of four or five layers per pallet. My cousin (three years older than me) had a more solid body than me; I struggled a bit, but we both got super fit (and super tired at the end of each day) very quickly. Sweating profusely, we would often share cold beer from a huge 1.5-litre bottle with our French comrades. Nobody ever got sick from it!

Obviously, as foreigners, with no French whatsoever, we were 'the niggers' to our work comrades and perhaps to most other locals, and this was (is) the harsh reality in most environments where immigrants arrive, work and settle, for a very long time. We assimilated well, even ending up in relationships with the local girls, mine lasting and surviving for many years ahead and becoming 'online' and continuing now, almost four decades later.

Money and the freedom of democracy appealed very much, despite the social awkwardness and stigma.

Driving, proudly, a newly purchased, old Peugeot car back home, to Poland, via Paris for a few days and nights (in the car!), handing over the car keys to my Dad as a 'thank-you gift', my mind was made up. I was going to be out of Poland for good, as soon as I could! Only this time, it was not a holiday plan, but a one-way ticket to an Austrian police station in Vienna and officially becoming a political refugee ...!

III.   THE FINAL EXIT

More passport/visa, trip-permit arrangements bound up in Communist red tape (I was now experienced and an expert at navigating it, even though still a teenager). I pretended this time that the reason for this trip was a 'family wedding'. After very prolonged, painful and tearful farewells and with parental blessing, a backpack of clothes, and $150 in my pocket, I left. Goodbye, not see you later –obviously this time was much different.

Handing myself over to the Austrian police at a Vienna city station was the first official step, notably with no return, as I was fingerprinted, photographed and my passport was taken away, never to be seen again. (Apparently, since a passport remains the property of the issuing authority of origin, it gets returned, promptly, via the official channels, back to where it came from – a confirmation signal to the homeland that the holder is no longer returning!) I was processed fairly quickly by the cops and transported into the main refugee camp on the outer peripheries of the Austrian capital city, where it all slowed down, or actually came to a grinding halt, amongst the tens of thousands of others, who had fled the Eastern European block and/or some other oppressed (African) nation.

Families with children were separated from the single men like me, and the barren, miserable camp life began, in huge dorms, with no furniture, holding triple-height steel bunks of some 30-40 men in each. Medical checks, immigration questionnaires (paper-based, of course!) and interviews, shared ablution amenities, three meals a day, sprinkled with some 'underground' evening porn movies in the attic, and various contraband cells trading in cigarettes, alcohol and drugs.

'Free' to come and go and return to one's bunk (I cannot remember any curfew) as you please, with a newly issued refugee ID and a few months later, once cleared by the Austrian Immigration department, a new Austrian photo ID-travel document, with a confirmation of the status of political refugee; giving one full social security, work and travel rights in and out of Austria. It was a privilege and quite an achievement at the time and under the circumstances because in some cases (previous criminal or political activity) deportation was a real threat to those who were there with any undesirable previous history.

I remember stories of some, who, unable to obtain a passport for one reason or another, escaped Poland by 'jumping the green border', over a river, a forest, chased by border patrols dogs – even being shot at.

Dad told me some years earlier he knew of cases where some desperate Poles had skated over the frozen Baltic Sea (or kayaked the same route in summer), Northbound to Denmark (Bornholm Island), or further on to Sweden! There would have been no such news reports ever broadcast in the tight-lipped, controlled media. Such a spectacular escape would have given the applicant a green light to refugee status, guaranteed. There were many others, who managed to wrangle a passport to leave the homeland, but were genuinely afraid of persecution/arrest upon return home, due to some trade union or political connections unfavourable with the communists, and this group was also given status to remain in the West with priority.

All who got to this stage knew their bridges were truly burned and down by becoming 'criminals' and traitors in the eyes of the authorities back home. The comfort was they were now allowed either to remain and work/study in Austria (or Germany, or any other free Western democracy offering asylum at the time) or apply to emigrate abroad, or overseas to any land afar, which was at the time accepting applications from refugees. Some chose to remain/relocate within Austria, some chose to apply to other West Euro destinations, and most, like me, applied overseas. In any case it was a tedious, time-consuming process, beginning with lots of paperwork, followed by many interviews (interrogations), proceeded by queuing outside the respective embassies, often overnight, sometimes for more than a day/night at the time, just to lodge forms and/or to be seen, as due to the numbers, no appointments were given. Vienna is so pretty, both in summer and in winter, snowed under. Pity 'you can't eat the scenery'– we were all penniless and often hungry! (Priorities were cigarettes and booze!)

While still a resident of the camp outside of Vienna, I scored a cheap, old vehicle from some young Poles who got accepted and were off to the USA. It was a large, sixties' model Opel Record station wagon, and I quickly turned it (or tried to) into a business enterprise. Potential Polish refugees were pouring into Austria at the time, either arriving at the Schwechat Airport or the Wien Hauptbahnhof train station, both a long way away from the camp. I would solicit the business by offering the newly arriving and scared Poles my local knowledge and a ride to the camp, which was otherwise a very expensive cab fare, for half price. Think Uber in the early eighties, but without any registration, permit, or an app. This soon pissed off the local taxi drivers, whose business was obviously suffering with this foreigner's approach. On one such occasion, my solicitation attempts were observed by the cabbies and I was physically kicked out of there, with 'don't let us ever catch you here again, you fucking Polish scumbag!'

Needless to say, I heeded the warning and never tried it again.

My campmates and I used the wagon, all of us drunk, one late night soon after, following stealing some top-up engine oil containers from the forecourt of a small gas station that was closed for the night. Petrified, under the influence of alcohol, and recklessly driving away from the crime scene, we crashed my wagon into a pile of potatoes out on a country road among the fields, and abandoned the vehicle, to never see it again. (At acquisition, I'd never bothered to transfer its registration into my name.)

While on the topic of crime among us, such ungrateful immigrants, the camps had lots of shady characters (to this day, I do not consider myself to be one of them, despite the admissions published here!) and it makes me wonder, if the combination of the circumstances, the psychological trauma and the young stupidity and bravado could be the contributors to such behaviour ... Ah!

I remember meeting a small gang (three or four) of well-dressed, swish, Hollywood-like young Poles, who were secretly introduced to me as specialists in obtaining anything at all; from clothing, smokes, booze, to electronics and even furniture and whitegoods; all brand new, per order, at a fraction of retail price, with three days' notice (and a deposit!). I was fascinated (never used their service, though), and without any planning, with two other mates late at night in Vienna's downtown quiet street, we carefully removed the whole front glass panel from a luxury winter clothing boutique. Alarm bells ringing, we quickly helped ourselves to as much as we could wear and carry – leaving running into the darkness. I wore my part of the loot for years to come; what shameful souvenirs. No guilt, as if Austria owed us.

I was lucky my cousin (the same one I worked and stayed with in France before), who did not choose to pull the pin on the motherland like me, 'the traitor', even among my own, was in Vienna at the time, labouring, with three of his Polish mates – a standard fare for the always entrepreneurial Poles, earning the hard foreign currency and returning home quadrupling (plus) the value of what they'd earned while slaving away in the West. Lawyers and other highly qualified professionals; labouring, tiling, cleaning, etc., to this very day, on their short 'expeditions', returning home wealthy heroes. (Winners?)

Having their company in Vienna gave me an opportunity to have some company outside of the camp and to socialise, wildly. Our parties included other Poles we'd met and some locals and other foreigners/tourists who were in Vienna at the time. Some of the newly formed relationships have lasted for many years, and some even ended up in marriages ... and divorces later.

Through one of those newly created contacts, I was befriended by a young Austrian/Portuguese couple with a young child, who were living in an inner-city apartment. Following some parties, we attended together in the city, they visited me in the camp soon after, and following some brief arrangements with the authorities and the camp management, took me in to stay with them, indefinitely. I was so lucky, now with an address in the centre of Vienna! We became best friends (thirty-seven years later, we are connected and chat, occasionally on Facebook, from opposite sides of the globe). I babysat their little child, cleaned, washed up, etc., while they were at work; and we cooked, ate, drank and smoked together. They spoke German and English, which not only gave them the opportunity for decent employment but also allowed them to mingle with the locals, giving them a broad range of friends. Us Poles didn't like the Austrians (and vice versa, the latter for more obvious reasons. After all, we were like the gypsies: cheap labour, usually not able to speak the lingo). We were the ones draining their economy, committing crime, taking their jobs and sometimes their women. Some things never change. This is still the case today, with refugees in the wider world out there. This social gap was not as much in my face then, but it surely broadened and is still, in some ways, in place today, almost four decades later, as I contemplate the subject of refugee settlement and assimilation … more on this later.

My new flatmates managed to help me with getting a job, just a short walk over the Danube Bridge. I was hired as an offsider, at a fresh flower distribution company, working alongside a van driver, a Serbian, who drove like a maniac, was a horny, perverted chauvinist who couldn't speak a word of English (only German, which apparently made him somehow superior to me) and a nice, softly spoken African manager, who also did not speak any English. Regardless of the fairly good wage I received and needed (not to mention my destitute flatmates who badly needed it too, which selfishly never occurred to me at the time), hating my job, I chucked it in only two to three months later! Such self-absorption certainly created some tensions between us at the flat.

It was a flamboyant lifestyle, with train trips to the Kiel Canal and Hamburg in Germany, where my Dad arranged a room for me, in the St. Pauli red-light district, with a Polish student who was there at the time. Or I would board my dad's ship, stay for the duration of the passage on board (from memory a couple of days), during which time I would have some great conversations with my wise father, over my possible destinations around the world to emigrate to, with fancy clothing and always booze and smokes eating up my Austrian dole-money.

I became familiar not only with Vienna but also with my rights and eligibilities there, as a recipient of political refugee and permanent residency status, and so I applied and received a generous income benefit (living and language-study allowances), which funded the setting up of my own flat with other three Poles and my girlfriend. It was away from downtown but with a fantastic public-transport network we all got to know very well, and we were able to get about without any problems 24 hours a day, seven days a week.

Life then was good in Vienna for me, after only the very recent experience of hunger, scavenging the city parks for firewood – including vandalising any wooden benches and other infrastructure in the rebellion and anger which was so unfounded towards this welcoming host country and city – and streets at night, for anything else that could be taken. At last, money was coming in, for nothing, with a nice place to live and party. A youngsters' paradise. And we still hated the Austrians, joked about their ways and never even attempted to blend into their society – language being the main barrier.

My applications to emigrate from Europe to the USA, Canada, South Africa, New Zealand and Australia were slowly progressing, and after several discussions while visiting my dad's ship in the Kiel Canal and Hamburg on global politics/economics, etc., my dad strongly advised for me to focus on NZ. I was actually accepted by both – the Kiwi and the South African governments at the same time, so with consideration given to apartheid rule and compulsory army service in South Africa, NZ was the go for me! I did not even give a proverbial blink, or look back on Europe, or Vienna (after living there for about one and a half years), as I packed my backpack for my Antipodean flight, courtesy of the Kiwi government (Robert Muldoon?) at the time.

IV. NEW LIFE

I never knew anyone in New Zealand, neither did I know anybody else in the group (20 odd) of other Poles on the flight Down Under.

All I remember is it was the longest one you can catch on earth! As the Poles do, we got very pissed throughout the three days and two nights on board and in transit lounges en route South East, against global time zones. It was my birthday and I celebrated it TWICE! We drunk the plane's bar dry!

Sure enough I made some good friends on board that flight: three of them were to become my best friends in New Zealand and Australia – one of them, like a brother, years later. (The photo below shows two of them.)

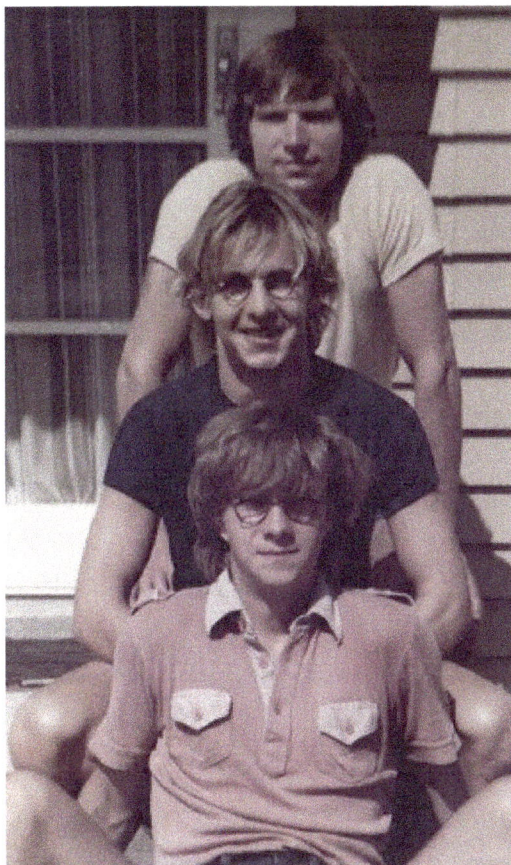

Image: NZ, circa 1983. Author at the bottom.

The refugee processing centre at the camp in South Auckland was very decent, although basic, obviously, but certainly unlike the cold-steel army style in Austria. It was a gated community; a handful of wooden houses of several single bedrooms each, shared amenities and some larger meeting/dining halls, plus some offices. (Interestingly this place is still operational, maintained by the New Zealand government today.) We were there only for a few days; it was pre-arranged that we got collected individually, or in smaller groups, by our local 'sponsors', who were the generous people of Aotearoa, mostly from church groups, who took us into their homes, open term and for no financial reward, spread out throughout the country. Mine was a young civil engineer, flatting with a group of five other singles (two males and three girls), under fairly strict, Christian house rules. Church on Sundays, no foul language and no sleeping together. We had lots of fun, laughter, playing music, sharing the cooking and housecleaning promptly. I have very fond memories there – my first 'real home' since leaving the motherland. We all became mates, our friendships lasting for many years, remotely and still existing online today.

I've always been a true 'Petrolhead', ever since I can remember, with a keen interest in the automotive. So in my job hunting, I decided to call myself a car mechanic. I was hired quickly by a local garage – those were the days of one applicant for one vacancy. I didn't last long, as the lack of real trade skills soon became obvious. After clumsily spilling some brake fluid on a lady's car in the forecourt, I was promptly sacked.

The first real job, came easy too. I was hired as an engineering department Storeman, in a large food manufacturing company. Further away from home, with no suitable public transport, getting to and from work became an issue. I was allowed to borrow my flatmate's 500cc Yamaha motorcycle a few times, but due to his safety concerns of me riding a large bike in a foreign country, on 'the other side of the road', it could not be a permanent arrangement. On the strength of my new job's wage, through a new contact in financial/accounting (Polish) circles in Auckland, I obtained a loan and bought myself a car: a 1275 Mini GT! 100 mph, no worries! And yes, it is true: it's not what you know but who you know – not a cliché.

The house-flatting was a hoot, the job was hassle-free and easy, compared to labouring at the port in France. I had my own car, my social life was good, between my Polish mates' visits (they ended up living some 100 km south) and frequent parties at 'my' place. It didn't take long, and my future wife arrived on the scene. A Kiwi girl of European descent, who became one of the flatmates. Following the house rules, on discovering our association, she was made to leave the house, on good terms and we soon ended up getting a place of our own. A year later our first son was born!

During this time, my older sister, who was only just newly married to a Polish seaman-radio operator, ended up in New Zealand. As per the plan, while in port (in Singapore, I think ...) he jumped ship and claimed political asylum (familiar?), requesting to be reunited with his wife in New Zealand! After some media coverage and our political lobbying, the request was granted and with the story making the international news, they began their own New Zealand residency, with my sister still there to this day. My brother-in-law passed away, peacefully, recently, leaving behind two handsome, intelligent and educated nephews of mine.

V.   DOMESTICATED

I became a car salesman, and we moved about a bit, as you do, and life in Auckland was good. Typically, we started to accumulate 'stuff' and there were more and more reasons to work longer hours and to earn more to support our expanding lifestyle. I guess with a local wife and network, I was finally and slowly becoming 'a local' ... for 'When in Rome, do as the Romans do'.

Australia has always been an attractive destination for Kiwis to go to, to work and live. Obviously, Oz has a much bigger population and economy, offering better wages and more opportunities. With a one-year-old first-born and no visa/work restrictions for New Zealanders, we took the plunge and went off to live in Perth, on the West coast – again on one-way tickets, in 1984!

I immediately scored a job selling cars, we rented an apartment with a pool – loved it there! Three/four months later, after meeting and talking with a cab driver, I took a week's training course and became a self-employed taxi driver. Hungry for money, spending twelve hours a night on the road, I soon became a 'gun', acquiring all the tricks of the trade, real-quick.

Two major road accidents over the course of four years (the first caused by a drunk driver, with passenger, tragically both deceased as a result, and the second by a stoned car thief) didn't put me off, and with generous monetary compensation from the Road Transport authorities, we ended up buying a nice house in the suburbs, and a couple of years later I bought my own taxi licence, making me now an owner-driver!

I am proud to this day, as I developed my own clientele, my cab being the first one in the history of the state to be equipped with a mobile phone and having its own credit-card processing facility (a manual portable printer – this was the eighties hi-tech!), and even my own business cards! My day driver and other colleagues in my network would cover the work and things were moving smoothly. The fear of industry deregulation was always clouding our business and its market value, but overall, it was an appreciating asset and consistently earning good cash with no official records of income.

As a young, handsomely attractive and 'successful' family, we made some good friends while living in Perth (wife was a cheerful sanguine/extrovert), becoming truly locals; yet, same as before, it was mainly mixing with other immigrants and foreigners. The local parish church provided most of our contacts, and we got to know the priest well. I was on the parish council, chaired in for two terms, became the top Mass reader and a special minister. Out roots were down and established.

Two more children were born to us in Perth. Living well, we took holidays to Europe, even venturing back to Poland, with the safety of Australian citizenship and Australian passports. I had no concerns, considering Poland was already free from the grasps of the Communist regime, partially thanks to the election of a Polish Pope in the Vatican and the widely accepted and popular Solidarity Party.

Driven by ambition and greed, we decided to take on more debt and went into property development, getting a parcel of land in a brand-new subdivision. Hiring an architect to design and to supervise the building of our new home was as flamboyant as it gets. Jarrah hardwood carpentry and floors, fancy brickwork with circular attic-windows, instant and reticulated lawns; and a few-long months later we moved into our immaculate, almost palatial seven-bedroom, two-kitchen, three-bathroom house, with a new Yamaha piano and plenty of space for us all.

Overcapitalising textbook material. Cringe! I can vividly remember, how we kept on overcommitting ourselves, by getting extra mortgage extensions from the bank, several times, basically living off credit and the ever-shrinking principal value of our property. (A friendly, Polish bank manager, ended up losing his job over our portfolio, unfortunately.)

I was a road-king-warrior in the taxi circles at the time but slowly got rather cocky, certainly complacent and somewhat lazy. Socialising over coffee and cigarettes with my cabbie mates regularly, I was spending too much time in cafes, rather than chasing work, on the road.

Interestingly, most of my mates were also foreign immigrants, 'wogs', and again, the criticising and joking about the locals and their 'lack of culture' was evident among us. Just like it was back in Austria and in France before. There is something in it, I wonder ...

Nightshift work and its clientele are much different from your '9-to-5 office job'! Sure, driving with very little traffic around has its advantages, but for a young, handsome man, mixing with the nightlife/workers certainly posed some temptations and risks ...

During the final year of my decade of taxi driving in Perth, I ended up snorting drugs, smoking and even drink-driving. Ashamed, I have never mentioned this to anyone before. Guilt set in! Obviously, I was no longer bringing any substantial money home and we found ourselves financially desperate.

Selling the taxi business (taxi licence plates in the pre-deregulation era gained much value over time) brought some short relief, but the writing was on the wall for us: we were doomed! Even a very generous friend's financial rescue of a sizable amount gifted to us, disappeared instantly, soaked up by the debt.

The house auction returned no result and we had to sell in desperation, at tens of thousands of dollars below cost. Painful and scarring. Over the following few months of renting, in between truck driving and casual gigs, we packed up and returned back to New Zealand. 'Bruised' and in tears.

Reestablishing again, we almost enjoyed the novelty of our fresh circumstances. I quickly scored a job — a 'dream job', really: a fellow parishioner, a good family man with a civil construction business and about a dozen staff hired me as a Yard/Storeman, and later a crane/truck & trailer operator, come coordinator, with a company vehicle – a cool autonomous role. Sadly, my tenure there lasted only two to three years, and due to a tough economy at the time and several sizeable debtors who never paid us, the firm was placed into liquidation and all the jobs were lost.

Our family assimilated well in a nice seaside location, enjoying good friendships, again, mainly through a local parish church, where we were involved and known by many. This time we were really locals and surrounded by locals, yet, some of my Maori work colleagues would joke of me, saying (softly), tongue-in-cheek: 'Oh ... look, these fucking foreigners, landing on our shores, taking our women, our jobs, even claiming our land'. Funny joke, but it still resonates, considering my immigrant past.

Later, after a couple of short-term gigs, I finally cracked it, job-wise! One of my sister's best friends, knowing I was job hunting in Auckland, arranged for me to meet her brother, who was a top-dog: President of the Union of Waterside Workers at the port.

I will never forget this meeting! It was at his downtown office, full of cigarette smoke, where we chatted, casually, for over an hour. An Irish mafia-like man, with a strong, distinctive accent. With a great knowledge of history and global events, a true statesman, he was reminiscent of the old days in Belfast, when he was a little boy, recalling how his father had a revolver gun at home and how he saw his father was roaming the streets of Belfast with his mates, 'shooting at the Catholics', while being shot at, all the same ... Colourful past ... Anyway, towards the end of our meeting, he picked up the phone, after telling me he was going to ring the HR Manager at the port. His tone, language full of expletives demanding for me to be hired, right there and then, no matter what! He ended his monologue, abruptly saying he was sending me over in fifteen minutes to sign the forms. Which I did, with shaky hands and following the usual recruitment process, with medicals, etc. I was duly a stevedore on the waterfront a couple of weeks later. And my life changed.

There was nothing like it, job-wise, to be employed on the waterfront, no matter the role. This is a subject matter for another book, there was just so much to it! I don't mean to say the work was complex — quite the opposite, but there was just so much to it historically, socially, politically, financially, personally ...

I cannot think of any other industry or a workplace with this much inertia and 'old rules'. Time-wise, this was to be the very last decade of strict trade-union reign and 100% workers' membership obedience in New Zealand (and to a certain degree globally, with not many ports around the world still with the union's fist in their face).

I was grateful to have scored the job, and by default became a union member from day one. It would have been unthinkable and unworkable for it to be otherwise. In stark contradiction to this, my previous stevedoring job on the French waterfront, given 'under the table' by the owner of the private firm, ended quite dramatically, when the local union sniffed out there were a couple of Poles taking *their* local members' jobs, and so we had to go!

It was a 'cruise on auto-pilot' gig in Auckland port, with the only effort given to be awake in a 24/7, hazardous environment, exchanging one's time for money, doing 'back to back' double shifts, often 60–70 hours per week. And much of it was downtime; standing by, no kidding. No efficiency, either! I heard many a story from my senior comrades that I missed the proverbial boat – that the real good times on the waterfront were some ten years back … with 'money for nothing' (and I thought we were still getting it!).

Despite my spending most of my time at work, we'd had three more children, built a huge, new house, always had two cars, more overseas holidays and lots of booze in between.

Fourteen years … It wasn't healthy and it wasn't good for us, as a family. With our six children, my wife of almost twenty years decided there was still enough 'fun' to be had ahead of her, and she demanded to end our marriage … I felt and was convinced my life had ended!

I was totally devastated, as I was 'sent packing', only with my clothes in suitcases and my car. She persuaded me, for the sake of the children and their home, that I had to go.

More booze, drugs, still at the port job, drifting, flatting, staying in cheap motels, sometimes sleeping in the car, or at work, I was a wreck.

I even failed at suicide. It took her only a few months of partying and not paying the bills, to lose our house to the bank's mortgage-forced sale. She moved with our children to rented accommodation, chucking all of our married-life memorabilia into a jumbo skip bin. A local real-estate agent bought our house from the bank; we got nothing and were penniless. Déjà vu. Slow learners.

Our separation and divorce were very messy, in fact it was ugly and militant, we were in combat mode against each other. The Inland Revenue Department made sure to take most of my wages I was still earning from my job and give it to her and to other solo mothers in the country, as the 'System' has it, which added to my despair. Tragically, I got duped and was also coughing up cash to her and the kids, unofficially (without record).

This lasted another four long years, until someone suggested I apply for a grant to do Outward Bound …

> Outward Bound, located in the Marlborough Sounds, at the top end of New Zealand's South Island. It helps you reach your full potential through challenge in the outdoors. The classrooms are the mountains, bush and waterways of this beautiful corner of NZ. Outward Bound is a non-profit organisation – their aim is to help create better people, better communities, and a better world. People of all ages, cultures, abilities and backgrounds are welcome at Outward Bound.
>
> All Outward-Bound courses are designed on these principles:
>
> **Learning through Experience** – learn by doing! Learn more about yourself and others from challenge, success and failure, self-reflection and feedback. All activities are designed to promote learning that can

be transferred to home and work. **Adventure and Challenge** – the courses are based on real adventure, where the participants have experiences that are physically, mentally and emotionally challenging. It will push your limits and help you conquer your fears! **Physical Activities in the Outdoors** – All activities involve situations where there are real consequences. All the staff, highly skilled instructors, deliver the courses, which include activities such as Sailing, Kayaking, High ropes, Rock climbing, Solo experience, Tramping, Physical training. You don't need any previous outdoors experience to participate. **Safe and Supportive Environment** – Clearly maintained boundaries ensure physical and emotional safety. Supportive relationships and culture. Outward Bound is not a destination it's a journey. Like every rewarding journey it's full of challenges. The experience of trying new things and being challenged builds confidence, resilience and helps develop new skills and behaviors (http://www.outwardbound.co.nz).

I had to give it the plug it deserves, as it truly was an unforgettable, life-changing experience and I wholeheartedly recommended it to anyone, be it a troubled teen, a midlife crisis stressed adult, to a senior looking for a kick!

Describing my miserable circumstances to the deciding panel, miraculously I was accepted and a generous corporate donor was found to bankroll my scholarship to the South Island Camp, where I was totally transformed, for life!

VI.   ANOTHER NEW LIFE

The Outward-Bound experience is subject matter for another book, suffice to say it totally blew my mind, changed and cleansed my life and still – I practice it, daily, to this day; taking care of self, others and the environment.

Soon after my 'OB' I joined a group and started motorcycle tours up and down both New Zealand islands, made some new friends and, after four years of being on my own, 'licking my wounds', I met a lovely Fijian-Chinese Kiwi woman (who had never been married and had no children before!), who became the mother of our son, a year later.

The political tensions between the trade union and the employer on New Zealand's waterfront scene became highly volatile, with strikes, lockouts and polarised public opinion; mostly against us, 'the lazy, overpaid wharfies', as we were called. It was discouraging and I was divided between the two opinion camps. During one of the long strikes, I was not prepared to stand at the barricades outside the port gates, yet I was certainly not prepared to let go the camaraderie and the affiliation I had with my union workmates, and to negotiate a filthy personal contract offered at the time to the striking workers; some of whom, betraying the union, took it up and became scabs for life. With fourteen years of good pay, some savings and a decent amount of superannuation, I decided to change my direction and signed up to become a full-time university student in IT instead.

In a bizarre show of power, tyranny and dictatorship, my employer resorted to hiring a private investigation firm and had me under surveillance, watching all my moves, when I was attending university classes, while I was claiming stress leave, which was legitimate on my part – caused by the ongoing strike action and our lock out from the work gates.

During the same period of time, I was also followed to and around a funeral I attended, some 100 km down the line from Auckland, of a dear old friend (he was the sponsor of my three Polish refugee mates, whom I met on the same flight from Austria to NZ, over thirty years prior). This was my employer's attempt to 'catch' me while on compassionate leave from work (three day's pay, thank you very much, for a union-negotiated contract!), which was such a waste of resources and so blatantly arrogant, nasty and unscrupulous of management. (I later found out from behind the scenes, it cost them over twenty thousand dollars for this surveillance!) Looking for 'blood' – this is how desperate they were to stamp out union membership, finding/fabricating anything they could, in this their 'union–employee eradication' campaign, regardless of the cost and the resources, since most, like me, had many years of valuable on-the-job experience.

We were, over time, replaced with the 'yes-men' (and women); a new breed of personnel, who never asked questions, did not belong to a trade union and who would always remain 'on-call', as per their new, casual (bastardised) employment contact. This process only took two to three years, and today only a handful of the 'old school' remain there, silently counting their days to retirement, dragging their chains, silenced by the 'new' climate, in this era of globalisation and labour arbitrage. For in this borderless, global economy, people around the world are free to travel and, with very few restrictions, work where they please. It is certainly a bonus for the developing nations and a chance for the often-poor immigrants to gain paid employment – a luxury they didn't have back home. And if a good job was offered, complete with a residency visa – bingo! What a bonus for both sides. On the other hand, it also causes misery in the local workforce, unable to compete, where the lowest bidder gets the job. This is evident, today, around Western and Scandinavian Europe, the UK, North America, Australia and New Zealand, with much political turmoil and pressure on the economy and public opinion.

But hang on ... isn't this a repeat of where I was at, in France and then in Vienna only a few years before ...? History repeating itself and human nature prevailing all the same. Who and what is fair ...?

> Globalization is not just continuing—it's accelerating. In 2020 there will be 40% more 25–34-year-olds with higher education degrees from Argentina, Brazil, China, India, Indonesia, Russia, Saudi Arabia, and South Africa than in all OECD countries (a group of 34 countries primarily in Western Europe and North America)(Taylor Pearson, The End of Jobs: Money, Meaning and Freedom Without the 9-to-5).

- End of jobs
- Gig economy
- New technology

- Labour arbitrage

- Globalised, borderless open market

- Robotisation, driverless transport, etc.

My own opinion:

The terminology above has been haunting us in recent years ...

Books have been written, talks given, articles published on the topic. Not only are we familiar with it; we have been thinking, debating, 'scheming', planning, how to outmanoeuvre this modern-day beast. But maybe, just maybe, it is just today's hype, delivered to us by the ever-sensational media and our own catastrophising ... Acknowledging that retaining, or getting, a job was different, very different in the past. It can also be suggested that today's employment trends may simply be a (natural) result of our interconnected, globally-open market, with all its advantages and disadvantages ...

Apparently, skill shortages still exist and even if robots will inevitably replace us in some jobs, someone will still have to make, code, supervise, control, maintain, recharge and clean the robots.

Also, most of us will always choose to have a PERSON cut our hair, babysit our children, provide us with medical care, professional advice, plus many other human touch, social interactions we as humans desire and constantly seek by our nature.

'No matter what happens ... somebody will find a way to take it too seriously.' – Dave Barry

In my case, the situation at the port job turned out so serious, the union lawyer was preparing the files to defend my case in court. On the last day of mediation, at the risk of the litigation costing the union a fortune in fees and my doctor pulling out of being my key witness, I also decided to pull the pin, let it go (get sacked) and sign to end my employment as a 'mutual agreement' to terminate, without any bad official record. Only the sour taste, at least in me ... Funny how the very young manager who had the task of sacking me, got fired some years later, for misuse of company funds.

Contradicting my spiel above, opinions on the topic of globalisation vary. According to some academics from the [McKinsey Global Institute](#):

> Low-skill labor is becoming less important as factor of production. Contrary to popular perception, only about 18 percent of global goods trade is now driven by labor-cost arbitrage. Three factors explain these changes: growing demand in China and the rest of the developing world, which enables these countries to consume more of what they produce; the growth of more comprehensive domestic supply chains in those countries, which has reduced their reliance on imports of intermediate goods; and the impact of new technologies.

Globalization is in the midst of a transformation. Yet the public debate about trade is often about recapturing the past rather than looking toward the future. The mix of countries, companies, and workers that stand to gain in the next era is changing. Understanding how the landscape is shifting will help policy makers and business leaders prepare for globalization's next chapter and the opportunities and challenges it will present. The decline in trade intensity is especially pronounced in the most complex and highly traded value chains. However, this trend does not signal that globalization is over. Rather, it reflects the development of China and other emerging economies, which are now consuming more of what they produce."

This makes sense. Our consumerism in developed/wealthy countries drives the economies of the developing nations, where the cheap goods are made, which in turn helps their middle class grow wealth, sufficiently turning them into consumers in their own local market. My guess is, the global economy will soon run out of places with cheap labour, which will inevitably force us to pay more, despite the promises by the likes of Tesla and co., that with greater market uptake the prices will eventually fall. And where will the stuff be made and by whom? Yeah, the robots, I hear you say.

> The full role of services is obscured in traditional trade statistics. First, services create roughly one-third of the value that goes into traded manufactured goods. R&D, engineering, sales and marketing, finance, and human resources all enable goods to go to market. In addition, we find that imported services are substituting for domestic services in nearly all value chains. In the future, the distinction between goods and services will continue to blur as manufacturers increasingly introduce new types of leasing, subscription, and other "as a service" business models. **Trade**

based on labor-cost arbitrage is declining in some value chains ...

As global value chains expanded in the 1990s and early 2000s, many decisions about where to locate production were based on labor costs, particularly in industries producing labor-intensive goods and services. Yet counter to popular perceptions, today only 18 percent of goods trade is based on labor-cost arbitrage (defined as exports from countries whose GDP per capita is one-fifth or less than that of the importing country). In other words, **over 80 percent of today's global goods trade is not from a low-wage country to a high-wage country**. Considerations other than low wages factor into company decisions about where to base production, such as access to skilled labor or natural resources, proximity to consumers, and the quality of infrastructure. The map of global demand, once heavily tilted toward advanced economies, is being redrawn—and value chains are reconfiguring as companies decide how to compete in the many major consumer markets that are now dotted worldwide. McKinsey estimates that emerging markets will consume almost two-thirds of the world's manufactured goods by 2025, with products such as cars, building products, and machinery leading the way. By 2030, developing countries are projected to account for more than half of all global consumption. These nations continue to deepen their participation in global flows of goods, services, finance, people, and data.

The biggest wave of growth has been happening in China. Previous MGI research highlighted China's working-age population as one of the key global consumer segments; by 2030, they are projected to account for 12 cents of every $1 of worldwide urban consumption. As it reaches the tipping point of having more millionaires than any other country in the world, China now represents roughly a third of the global market for luxury goods. In 2016, 40 percent more cars were sold in China than in all of Europe, and China also accounts for 40 percent of global textiles and apparel consumption. As consumption grows, more of what gets made in China is now sold in China. This trend is contributing to the decline in trade intensity. The rising middle class in other developing countries is also flexing new spending power. By 2030, the developing world outside of China is projected to account for 35 percent of global consumption, with countries including India, Indonesia, Thailand, Malaysia, and the Philippines leading the way. In 2002, India, for example, exported 35 percent of its final output in apparel, but by 2017, that share had fallen by half, to 17 percent, as Indian consumers stepped up purchases.

Growing demand in developing countries also offers an opportunity for exporters in advanced countries. Only 3 percent of exports from advanced economies went to China in 1995, but that share was up to 12 percent by 2017. The corresponding share going to other developing countries grew from 20 to 29 percent. In total, advanced economies' exports to developing countries grew from $1 trillion in 1995 to $4.2 trillion in 2017. In the automotive industry, Japan, Germany, and the United States send 42 percent of their car exports to China and the rest of the developing world. In knowledge-intensive services, 45 percent of all exports from advanced economies go to the developing world. The Asia–Pacific region is already a top strategic priority for many Western brands. Technology can transform some products and services, altering the content and volume of trade flows in the process. For example, McKinsey's automotive practice estimates that electric vehicles will make up some 17 percent of total car sales globally by 2030, up from 1 percent in 2017. This could reduce trade in vehicle parts by up to 10 percent (since EVs have many fewer moving parts than traditional models) while also dampening oil imports.

The shift from physical to digital flows that started years ago with individual movies, albums, and games is now evolving once again with streaming and subscription models. Streaming now accounts for nearly 40 percent of global recorded music revenues. Cloud computing uses a similar pay-as-you-go or subscription model for storage and software, freeing users from making heavy capital investments in their own IT infrastructure. (https://www.mckinsey.com/featured-insights/innovation-and-growth/globalization-in-transition-the-future-of-trade-and-value-chains).

I felt odd, initially. After all, I had spent 14 years of my life there (at the port), my longest tenure thus far, doing the hours equivalent to two jobs ... and it cost me my family and almost my life. But I was now a full-time university student, with much work to do between lectures, assignments and self-study. Tertiary education is hard work; they don't give away bachelor's degrees for nothing – I can attest to this! Fortunately, I was financially secure, at least for now, with some savings, some government subsidies to study and most importantly, a caring new wife and the loving environment of my new family – 'Us3', as we call ourselves to this day.

I became fascinated with new technology! Some of the new stuff I learned, included the '**Internet of Things**' (**IoT**), which is described in an article posted on TechTarget/IoTAgenda in July 2013 (how time 'flies') as:

> ... a scenario in which objects, animals or people are provided with unique identifiers

and the ability to automatically transfer data over a network without requiring human-to-human or human-to-computer interaction. IoT has evolved from the convergence of wireless technologies, micro-electromechanical systems (MEMS) and the Internet.

A 'thing', in the Internet of Things, can be a person with a heart monitor implant, a farm animal with a biochip transponder, an automobile that has built-in sensors to alert the driver when tire pressure is low -- or any other natural or man-made object that can be assigned an IP address and provided with the ability to transfer data over a network. So far, the Internet of Things has been most closely associated with machine-to-machine (M2M) communication in manufacturing and power, oil and gas utilities. Products built with M2M communication capabilities are often referred to as being 'smart'.

IPv6's (yes, apparently it is coming, so is Christmas...) huge increase in address space is an important factor in the development of the Internet of Things. According to Steve Leibson, who identifies himself as 'occasional docent at the Computer History Museum', the address space expansion means that we could 'assign an IPV6 address to every atom on the surface of the earth, and still have enough addresses left to do another 100+ earths'. In other words, humans could easily assign an IP address to every 'thing' on the planet. An increase in the number of smart nodes, as well as the amount of upstream data the nodes generate, is expected to raise new concerns about data privacy, data sovereignty and security. Although the concept wasn't named until 1999, the Internet of Things has been in development for decades. The first Internet appliance, for example, was a Coke machine at Carnegie Melon

University in the early 1980s. The programmers could connect to the machine over the Internet, check the status of the machine and determine whether or not there would be a cold drink awaiting them, should they decide to make the trip down to the machine.

Kevin Ashton, co-founder and executive director of the Auto-ID Centre at MIT, first mentioned the Internet of Things in a presentation he made to Procter & Gamble. Here's how Ashton explains the potential of the Internet of Things:

Today computers – and, therefore, the Internet – are almost wholly dependent on human beings for information. Nearly all of the roughly 50 petabytes (a petabyte is 1,024 terabytes) of data available on the Internet were first captured and created by human beings by typing, pressing a record button, taking a digital picture or scanning a bar code.

The problem is, people have limited time, attention and accuracy – all of which means they are not very good at capturing data about things in the real world. If we had computers that knew everything there was to know about things – using data they gathered without any help from us – we would be able to track and count everything and greatly reduce waste, loss and cost. We would know when things needed replacing, repairing or recalling and whether they were fresh or past their best. (http://whatis.techtarget.com/definition/Internet-of-Things)

Since my Outward-Bound experience, four years prior, I was now a daily practitioner of conscious mindfulness and gratitude. My new family life was good, and our little baby boy was growing up in peace and harmony. Thanks to some professional mental health therapy I received, guided by a female psychologist, I mustered sufficient willingness and inner strength to call a meeting with my ex-wife, rid myself of (most of) the chauvinism and found FORGIVENESS! It was now fourteen years since we'd separated ... Call me a slow learner! All of a sudden, I was liberated, and all the hate and resentment lifted! Clarity, peace and contentment – all through forgiveness! I highly recommend it to anyone!

Needless to say, my six 'Poopsies' felt relieved too, noticing very quickly the big difference in their divorced parents becoming civilised towards one another, with decent communication, for a change.

In my third year at university in Auckland, NZ, I applied for an international study exchange and got accepted into a master's level IT program, for a full semester, at a university near the Danish capital, just outside of Copenhagen. Again, my project-planning skills and organisational ability from the early days in Poland and in Austria helped tremendously in making all the arrangements, and our family of three were off to Europe for seven months!

From the other side of the globe, via the internet, we were set with a new car lease, an apartment close to my uni and we even managed to have it semi-furnished, connected to all the utilities, with two mobile phone SIM cards posted to us in NZ just before we were due to depart! All this with no prior contacts in Denmark! The power of the internet is truly amazing, making this really such a small world.

My elderly parents, still living in Northern Poland, were my target of this exercise too, benefiting from our European relocation, however temporary. I held all my plans a secret from them; it was my dad's eightieth birthday coming up during this time, before our departure from NZ, so I made some online enquiries and organised a surprise birthday party at a new, flash, international hotel complex, near where Mum and Dad live. My auntie (Dad's youngest sister), while sworn to secrecy, invited the whole extended family. We checked into our room a day before the party. One of my older sons, who was visiting Europe at the time, also came to stay with us and at a certain time, when all guests had arrived, I appeared with my family in front of my parents. Tears of joy – it was a hoot!

When we first touched down in Europe, collecting our new car in Frankfurt, we drove to Prague, spent a couple of days there and approached the Polish border from the South, across the picturesque Tatra Mountains and Zakopane – a tourist's gem, up high in the mountains. Normally a skiing resort, this was in summer, so it was green and sunny. A drive across Poland, from the deep south, to the Baltic coast, is about 1000 km, so we took several days, visiting some cousins and being tourists, of course! My Chinese-Fijian born wife from New Zealand was in her element, fascinated with the history and the scenery, not to mention the shopping and the cuisine! Our little son was a perfect road-tripper and companion, never missing a beat, observing and commenting on everything very eloquently for his age (seven).

Following my Dad's big birthday party, after a few days spent at my old home with my parents, showing my wife and two sons around my old turf (my old primary school, my college, and the city where I was born and roamed around as a kid), we took a road trip I mapped out months before. We headed west from Poland, through Germany, via the port of Rostock and a car ferry to Denmark/Copenhagen. Later, more exotic road trips were to be enjoyed from our place in Denmark, during school holidays.

One such trip was to Bornholm Island, in the middle of the Baltic Sea, which very much reminded me of the coastal towns in Poland. Coincidentally, there were many Polish tourists there, via a regular ferry connection between Gdynia/Gdansk and Bornholm.

Another was far north, up across Sweden, where we visited a Kiwi couple (he was one of the old flatmates in my first house in Auckland) living there, en route to the Atlantic Road and the fiords around Molde, in Northern Norway. A truly fantastic experience, never to be forgotten!

Just like the trip we took to Reykjavik, Iceland, during the winter break from university. We spent a few days up there, over the New Year period. My favourite destination, ever! We even saw U2's Bono, casually strolling the streets of downtown Reykjavik one sunny, cold afternoon! Staying there was just magic. Making sure I always carry my running gear in my luggage (since Outward Bound), I find a real connection with a place going for my morning jog, even through the snow and ice that far north! (It wasn't that cold there, just hovering around zero Celsius.) Booze is expensive, but we agreed that with jobs in place we would happily live there! Dream on ... there is hardly any grass there for it to be greener than 'the other side' ... Besides, in my experience, it would be hard to beat living in the Antipodes! (I say this to myself every time I get 'itchy feet'! And it works!)

My studying in Copenhagen was different from New Zealand, perhaps obviously. Hard work, of course (this was master's level stuff!), but it always had this 'holiday' feel to it for me. Cycling to and from, even in the snow, was sometimes an uphill battle in more ways than one. Among my extra-curricular activities, I attended a very interesting business-incubator program in Copenhagen, called The Future Entrepreneurs of Denmark. It lasted most of the semester.

Future Entrepreneurs of Denmark (FED) is a diverse talent network that was established to bridge the gap between companies, the academic world and entrepreneurs. The network is a joint initiative of student organizations from numerous top universities in Denmark with focus on entrepreneurship.

FED equips students with a diverse, multidisciplinary network, practical and theoretical skills and know-how in order to have the necessary tools to utilise entrepreneurial opportunities and turn business ideas into reality. Each semester, the brightest and most talented students with diverse educational backgrounds are admitted into the FED programme.

In collaboration with top-tier partners such as Google, DesignIt, McKinsey & Company and many more, they develop the entrepreneurial mindset and competencies of the selected students through six exclusive and customized workshops and a final startup weekend (https://www.facebook.com/fednetwork/).

I found the program to be intense, challenging and very insightful! Proud to have been admitted and to complete the challenge (and I have a certificate to prove it!)

The university I attended in Denmark was absolutely full of foreign exchange students (our little son attended an international primary school in town, with a mix of foreign children, taught in English – wait for it – by a Kiwi and an Aussie teacher!), so I never felt like a misfit there. I must admit though, that our socialising as a family was again restricted only to immigrants (adults, who worked there, moved there, or had a local spouse, etc.). Denmark in particular, we found, was very exclusive socially and the locals were predominantly introverted, self-absorbed and closed, with no eye contact. I am absolutely certain; this would be a tough place for any refugee to settle in! Seemingly, a huge social gap remained open, and we were glad we were only there for a few months.

On a lighter note, alcohol consumption in Denmark is allowed on public transport and in outdoor public spaces. A cultural complement to how well behaved and civilised their drinking (in most of Western Europe) really is. Beer is cheaper than bottled water in any local grocery shop! How bizarre that it is also sold in petrol stations, including spirits, around most of Europe.

My exams were serious but conducted in a friendly, professional and respectful manner by the uni staff – mostly PhD fellows, who were students themselves, not so long prior. No concessions for an Aussie (with grey/receding hair), like me, though ... All four subjects had both written and oral 'defence' components. One subject, Robot Programming Architectures, included the presentation of a robot, built by oneself, in the weeks preceding the test. It had to do 'something'. Mine followed a line, turned left, turned right and then stopped, before reversing. Passed all! Woohoo!

In many ways we were glad to leave Europe for the Antipodes, at least for the weather, if not for the culture – being so rigid, stiff and obviously deep-rooted, historically, in Europe, compared to New Zealand and Australia. It does pay to be aware of this, my observation, based now on some thirty-five years of experience, before you throw a dart on a world map, in deciding where to live next. For the grass ain't greener on the other side – and you can't eat the scenery. And every postcard is made to look pretty.

The most significant piece of writing during my tertiary studies was, without doubt, the capstone project, the final piece of IT contemplation, which all had to be backed up with references, experiments and data, as well as 'defended' in person, in front of a panel of examiners. This is what I wrote about steganography for this project:

Steganography is the science of hiding secret data within an innocent carrier file, for storage and transfer in computer networks, providing the privacy of **invisibility** that is unattainable by cryptography.

It evolved from primitive methods in the early history of humankind to sophisticated methodologies in modern digital forensics and utilises different algorithms, depending on the file format, size and the desired level of **concealment**.

There are well over a hundred free-source tools available to perform steganography and to discover/undo the steganography process (steganalysis), with many complexities and shortcomings in this field, so often exploited by criminals to obscure their ill intentions.

Four identified objectives:

Objective 1

To hash all files before and after hiding data and to compare hash values. In order to achieve this objective, the following steps have to be taken:

— Encrypt a carrier file using any of the available encrypting tools and then check its hash value.

— Using steg Tool A ('S-tool'), hide the data in a carrier file. Then encrypt the carrier file (as in the step above) and check its hash. Repeat the same for Tool B.

— Use any Hex editing tool to analyse the carrier file before and after hiding data and locate changes, if any.

— Observe and record the outcome.

Objective 2

Using Tool A, attempt to reveal hidden data from a file done by using Tool B, reverse the operation, note the findings.

Objective 3

Search the internet for at least five carrier files that have data hidden in them and attempt to reveal the hidden data using appropriate steganalysis Tools A and B, ensuring to find files that Tools A and B can process in terms of format and size.

Objective 4

Analyse and document how each tool used hides data, i.e. which technique it employs: insertion or substitution.

Methodologies:

Various stego algorithms exist, designed specifically to manipulate certain types of file formats. Generally, it is all about mixing/hiding data within a decoy file (carrier), without disturbing its contents visually, in a way that it is inconspicuous to the human eye.

The outcome can be deciphered by employing the **same tool** used to hide the information at the source, or by a steganalysis tool, which, if used according to the type of file on hand, will at least indicate that there is something hidden within, or reveal the secret message to the recipient/investigator at destination.

File compression makes it difficult for steganography because it utilises the redundant, insignificant, 'white-noise'/'junk' bits of a file to its advantage, which is exactly the same area where hidden data is placed.

Lossy compression (as in JPEG, MP3/WAV, etc. files) saves space, but it strips the important elements (noise) that steganography needs for its own purposes, as well as affecting the integrity of the original file.

Lossless compression (in GIF, BMP, etc. files) is favoured by the stegano tools to hide data, but it is not used as commonly in data transfers/storage because while it retains most of the original detail, it requires much volume/space when implemented.

One of the methods used in steganography is the replacing (**substitution**) of the **Least Significant Bits** (LSB) of a file with hidden data. This can be done either in the comment field of the file header (in Invisible Secrets) or adding it (**insertion**) at the end of the file (like in SecurEngine).

Some tools, like Outguess, insert the data into redundant bits of the cover image by using frequency counts, others use graph-theoretic methodology to perform stego-hiding, like StegHide.

Another methodology used is to embed (secret data) in the carrier byte-stream, in a block/linear, sequential/fixed way (Jsteg, InPlainView), or by spreading, in a pseudo-random way, depending on the password (BMPSecrets, Steganos for BMP).

Also, it can be done by changing some bits of a carrier file, but avoiding any modifications to the statistical properties, so that it compensates for the alterations induced.

All tools chosen were free source and/or trial versions. (http://scholar.google.com / and http://en.wikipedia.org)

The reverse tool tests showed discrepancies, which may have been due to varying algorithms used by the distinct tools and also their limitations when exposed to files which were originally manipulated by different methodologies.

When steganalysis tools/techniques are used and file comparisons are available, it is usually possible to discover and to identify the **existence** of hidden data in a carrier message, but it is not necessarily possible to retrieve it. In order to achieve partial or full recovery, one must have the knowledge of what steganography technology was implemented in the first place. Most stega secrets are encrypted beforehand, adding to the complexity of recovery.

The availability of both – the original and the steganographic files makes it possible to compare file data attributes, file size/format, by analysing the hash/checksum values and any modifications to hex values, with time stamps, etc. in determining the existence of a hidden message, but this is a luxury not normally afforded to a steganalyst– forensic investigator.

It is by comparing the digital fingerprints of files, revealing some anomalies/discrepancies between the original and suspect file(s) that may allow for steganalysis to have any success. Without this comparison of the digital relationship between the object files, according to Ibrahim (2007), it is not possible to make comparisons of attributes between the original and suspect file; therefore, evidence would be difficult to verify or validate and prove inculpatory.

In his paper, Ibrahim mentions studies performed by researchers over twelve years ago, examining over **two million images** on the internet – without any success in identification of stega/hidden images and indeed pointing to a possibility that the currently available detection techniques may be inadequate against methods used in covert/hidden messages, or that images/files with hidden data are not as widely available, or not published on the internet as was erroneously thought ...

Ibrahim's report reveals that any success of steganalysis hinges on the availability of the stego-object(s), knowledge and availability of the stego algorithm used, availability of the original carrier and the presence of the combination of the above.

Another example of this (the unsuccessful detection of any hidden messages in images widely available on the internet), is the **scanning cluster**, performed on **one million images**, by Neils Provos, a German steganalysis scientist, where no covert data was found, confirming that any use of steganography on the internet is still very limited, if not at all (Krenn, 2004).

(In conclusion) on the methods used by different tools in the experiments, the variety of algorithms and their advancements over the years have helped in the effectiveness of steganography techniques and its detection (steganalysis).

A combination of same/specific methods and a secret key (known at both ends) must be used to have any success in recognition/detection of the existence and in attempting to analyse hidden information, which, as mentioned earlier, is not used much in the public arena on the Internet, as was erroneously thought.

Problems with the stego-tools noted in the experiments suggest some of the free-source programs available remain troublesome, as they are projects and work in progress themselves ...

It is certain that in the era of rising terrorist activity (as well as other criminal activity), globally, the digital forensics researchers will bring more advances in this field of computer science very soon, making it a fascinating, promising and a rewarding career path for today's IT graduates.

This is not comprehensive/extensive research, so the information presented here does not make it possible to determine with certainty about the state of stego and steganalysis tools, or if indeed, they perform to user expectations. Steganalysis tools inevitably fail when used with files they were not specifically designed to handle, as there is no universality or uniformity amongst them. As vague as it may appear, this view is shared by the experts in their writings referred to in this paper (Guillermito, 2004; Ibrahim, 2007; Judge, 2001; Krenn, 2004).

The detection, and furthermore extraction, of any hidden data rely heavily on many factors, which often cannot be overcome, simply with a naked eye, or by applying a software tool.

So far, the research results are not encouraging (Ibrahim, 2007; Krenn, 2004) and much will still have to be explored and achieved in this field before we can say with any certainty that covert digital data can be found and extracted successfully with the methodology and the tools available on hand ... [T.Z., November–January 2014–2015].

Mumbo jumbo maybe but, still, not too shabby for a political refugee, with English as a second language! Of course, I'm proud, just like I was a few years prior, when I got an A grade pass in English from Cambridge University in the UK (via distance education from New Zealand in 1983), when my sister (a qualified medical doctor at the time), scored a B+ for the same exam!

VII.   RETROSPECT

An integral part of my reflection on this social *événement* of global migration, regardless of reason, is my recent (June/July 2018) 'Big Loop Ride Australia'; my solo circumnavigation ride around the continent of Australia; 20,400 km under the stars, with no support, over a period of eight weeks (it took two years to research and plan this), in my attempt to find serenity and 'space' for contemplation. But I couldn't see any of it, even in such a vast space as Australia! Some say it is because I never went off-road and into the bush. (How could I? I was on a road bike!) Many 'experts' (or keyboard warriors) say you must venture off the beaten track, away from the highways, to feel 'the space'. Well, maybe, to a certain extent, in some overcrowded countries this may be true, but in Australia?!

During my (road) ride, I met and spoke to many globetrotters, 'grey nomads' as we call them, Down Under, who, like myself, drive/ride this huge land seeking something. And the main message was that there is no solitude 'out there', unless you have it, within … Many have recalled, how travelling across the deserted land, off-road and rough, after finding a great/picturesque secluded spot, by a waterhole or with views, they'd set up camp early, only to be surrounded by other campers later who also wanted a piece of the paradise for themselves, regardless. Public land; you cannot claim it as your own … And there goes your peace you were seeking.

From my ride blog in 2018:

Image: My Big Loop Ride @Australia. From Brisbane, anti-clockwise, 20,400 km solo.

Mission: to highlight the forgotten value of **silence, in my own company**, as some people can no longer enjoy self, away from the rabble of the crowd and the screen. Plan: to ride a motorcycle, solo, right around the continent, including Alice Springs and Uluru. Scope: ten weeks, 20,000kms, tent camping, no support crew. Purpose: to face the vastness/openness/loneliness, with self. Target: the modern, often displaced society adults and adolescents, with their relentless need of the 'busy' company of others and the dislike of one's own self in the silence of nature's space. The Story: realising similar rides have been done, many times before (I've read the blogs, books, watched the videos, know people who have done it, etc.), and as an experienced long-distance and commuter motorcyclist, I am putting a new spin on it, by contemplating human nature in the setting described above ... This ride was six years in the planning, following several rides up, down and across both islands of New Zealand that I have done, mainly in groups, over the last decade.

I was inspired by a friend, Mike Hyde, who described his own experiences in three _Twisting Throttle_ books, after he rode around New Zealand, Australia and America. I have ridden with Mike on his 'shorter' rides; 'Twisting Throttle' 2000 km in 48 hours, crossing from the East to the

West coasts and back, in the deep south of New Zealand.

Sadly, Mike passed away, peacefully, in August 2015, following a short illness.

As we are constantly surrounded by the noise of the crowd and the screens of our devices, many cannot handle a moment alone, in silence. That awkward minute with a stranger in the elevator, or a pause in a conversation with a newly met acquaintance. If we don't like ourselves, how can we be 'good company' to others ...?

Budget: Details available on request.

To deliver **value**, by the way of blogging/writing, photography, filming, advertising, etc. As for the **relevance** ... the sky (the Internet) is the 'limit' since I am addressing issues affecting today's society, globally. My potential supporter(s) will have a great(er) following than me and benefit from my experiment and reporting, with the value it will deliver to their stakeholders …

Veni, vidi, vici. Well … not really.

Off I rode and I did it. 'Knocked the bastard off', like Sir Edmund Hillary said of his much greater achievement compared to mine … (https://biglooprideaustralia.blogspot.com/2018/06/quo-vadis.html).

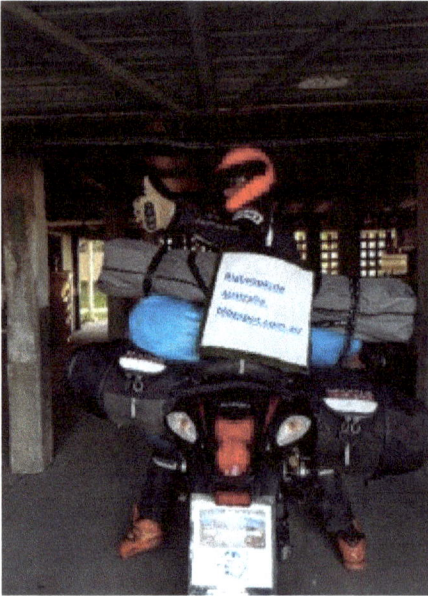

I did not find what I was looking for … And I am not quoting a song here! And I did not say 'unfortunately', either! Certainly, I'm proud of my ride and my whole journey to where I am at right now, since leaving my homeland and all that followed, as briefly alluded to above.

Stopping short of asking myself if I'd do it again, I am grateful for a life full of adventure, lessons, people who came my way, and most importantly, my family, especially my seven children. With so much more ahead, God allowing, one never stops wondering what's ahead. More so, as a job seeker, currently (2019), I, for the most part, feel much anxiety, considering my future, even tomorrow/next week/next month. For I may still have some fifteen years of work ahead of me, in whatever profession I choose … Or do I?

As a 'recent' graduate, with a Bachelor of Computing Systems degree (April 2016), I just came to the realisation – after receiving rejection after rejection while applying for jobs, over the last three years – at the age of 56, I have now become unemployable! I admit I haven't played my cards right, in more ways than one, especially since my uni study. I never bothered gaining work experience in the IT field, even if it took doing voluntary gigs! Realising it is a common phenomenon for job seekers of my vintage, I am one of many, 'out there', but I also know I have become an 'oddball' for recruiters and hiring managers. With almost four decades of work/life experience globally AND a new computing degree – but no IT industry work experience, nobody knows where/how to place me into the workforce. I must not let desperation decide and end up forgoing my degree by taking 'anything going', but must admit I have not received any offers and have been rejected even for truck and bus driving jobs I applied for in recent months … WTF? This has been a sobering experience that has made me become realistic … and cynical, at the same time. Recruitment is broken.

This reminds me of a school newsletter note, from a local principal:

1703 'Students today can't prepare bark to calculate their problems. They depend on their slates which are more expensive. What will they do when the slate is dropped and it breaks? They will be unable to write.'

1815 'Students today depend on paper too much. They don't know how to write on a slate without getting chalk dust all over themselves. They can't clean a slate properly. What will they do when they run out of paper?'

1907 'Students today depend too much upon ink. They don't know how to use a pen knife to sharpen a pencil. Pen and ink will never replace the pencil.'

1928 'Students today depend upon ink from a shop. They don't know how to make their own. When they run out of ink they will be unable to write works of cyphers until their next trip to town. This is a sad commentary on modern education.'

1941 'Students today depend on these expensive fountain pens. They can no longer write with a straight pen and nib. We parents must not allow them to wallow in such luxury to the detriment of learning how to cope in the real business world which is not so extravagant.'

1950 'Ballpoint pens will be the ruin of education in our country. Students use these devices and then throw them away. The values of thrift and frugality are being discarded. Business and banks will never allow such expensive luxuries.'

1980 'You can't use those calculators on the test. If I let you do that, you wouldn't ever learn how to use the tables in the back of the book and use interpolation to figure out your trig ratios.'

1989 'We can't let them use calculators in middle school. If we do, they'll forget how to do long division or how to multiply three-digit numbers by three-digit numbers. What will they do when they don't have access to a calculator?'

1995 'Why would you ever want the internet for student use? It's just the latest fad – have them use the library.'

1996 'You don't need a web page for our school. Who's ever going to look at it? Teachers will never use email.'

1999 'Why do you want network drops at every teacher's desk? You're not thinking of getting a computer for all of them, are you?'

1999 'What can you do with an LCD Projector that you can't do with an overhead projector?'

2000 'Why are we talking about students having laptops in school? I don't think most parents will even give their kids their old computer, much less buy them a new one.'

2001 'Why would I want to put my grades on the web? Who's going to look at them?'

2004 'Who could ever be bothered with texting, when you can just pick up the phone and call?'

2008 'Why would we use interactive whiteboards, when we can do the same thing with an overhead projector?'

2014 'Why would students need to have their own device as a learning tool, they use them now as a toy just to play games?' (From a school newsletter, P. Zernike, March 2019)

But seriously ... what is our school system teaching our next generation ...?

Is our curriculum adequate for the twenty-second century and beyond ...?

Many vivid examples exist, observing Generation Y and even prior, suggesting our schools are not gauging the students adequately and are not teaching the real-life and astuteness topics of:

- relationships, human interaction

- empathy

- budgeting, finance, borrowing, lending, equity, mortgaging, MONEY

- patience, consistency, planning

- delayed gratification (as opposed to instant)

- appreciation of the elderly, the history, the natural-beauty

- the value of silence (stillness)

- spirituality

- and much more

Our testing/exam structures are questionable; what really gets revealed in a 30-minute, or even a two-hour test, on a particular, good or bad, day for an individual, after a semester, or a year of study ...?

The more we question this status quo, the more obvious it becomes, that a real revolution in education is upon us.

In my case, it is not the education but the recruitment process that's 'gone broke' ...

Thinking some more ...
'The act or faculty of perceiving,

*or apprehending by means of the
senses, or of the mind; cognition; understanding
'....*

(http://www.dictionary.com/browse/perceptio
n)

I was asked, recently, for advice on a subject I
am very familiar with.

It was contrary to the recipients own beliefs and
so they openly asked for me to 'change their
perception' on the topic.

Needless to say, I backed out. Here is why:

Perception ... It comes <u>from</u> your **mind**. A
product/result of <u>your</u> **thinking**, which comes
from <u>your</u> **brain**.

<u>You own it!</u>

You control it (hopefully) and the external
circumstances, or at least, other people
shouldn't!

We have all heard before, that 'Happiness
comes from within' ...

Let's take it further, though: the outcomes, our results, originate (as ideas, put into action) in our brain!

This is a very powerful notion and if applied constantly and selflessly, in our dealings with each other and in whatever life throws at us, the world around us (careers, relationships, business, etc.) will be shaped according to our choices, plans/goals and our aspirations.

Take ownership of your results by altering your mind, objectively, with empathy and concern for others. And so, I am. I do, or at least I try.

Perhaps I've been a dreamer? Still chasing the rainbow ...?

I took this test, recently;

Here are my 'what job would make you happiest' scores:

> 1)   Creative use of ideas, materials or situations:

Your ideal work is mainly about working imaginatively with ideas or designs. This includes jobs in the arts, performing, creative writing, and also visual design, lateral thinking, business creativity, adapting or coming up with new ideas, working in situations where **no rulebook** exists. Example jobs include: graphic designer, training consultant, wedding planner, public relations.

2)   Supporting people:

Your ideal work is mainly about working with people, with their wellbeing and development as the main focus of your work. Example jobs include: teacher, life coach, therapist, nurse, learning and development, career coach.

3)   Making new things happen:

Your ideal work is mainly about achieving things with and through other people. This may involve organisational change, planning, managing projects, leadership, creating a new business, shaping teams, getting results. Example jobs include: project manager, team leader, operations manager, sales manager, business developer.

4)   Information and research, processes and systems:

Your ideal work is mainly about researching or managing information. This will include analysis, cataloguing and database management, but may include investigating topics in depth, IT, science, maths, quality control, systems and regulations. Example jobs include: accountant, scientific researcher, investigative journalist, legal assistant, book-keeper, health and safety officer, purchasing professional.

5)   Influencing, negotiating, communicating:

> Your ideal work is mainly about persuading other people to do something, buy something or believe in your cause. This includes driving others, influencing, persuading, lobbying, motivating, selling. Example jobs include: sales person, recruiter, fundraiser, event manager, estate agent, public speaker (https://www.theguardian.com/lifeandstyle/2014/nov/11/-sp-questionnaire-what-job-would-make-you-happiest).

Whatever …

This is another test I took (I even paid money for it!):

> The Enneagram Institute Riso-Hudson Enneagram Type Indicator (RHETI v2.5)

> Test Taker: Tom Zed

> Email Address: tom.zed@outlook.com

> Date of Test: 2018-09-05 UTC

Results Overview

Your highest score was for:

Type 1

Your second highest score was for:

Type 4

Your third highest score was a tie between:

Type 8, Type 3, Type 7

Enneagram Type Score

Type 1, The Reformer 22

Type 4, The Individualist 19

Type 8, The Challenger 17

Type 3, The Achiever 17

Type 7, The Enthusiast 17

Type 5, The Investigator 15

Type 2, The Helper 15

Type 6, The Loyalist 12

Type 9, The Peacemaker 10

Your primary Enneagram personality type is most likely the highest of these scores, and almost certainly among the highest two or three.

For additional information, you may want to read How to Interpret your Results, and consult our Misidentifications section for help with comparing the types.

You may also find it helpful to go over your test results and the personality descriptions with someone who knows you well.

Ultimately, there is no substitute for self-reflection. Please carefully read the Expanded Type Descriptions of your top types and reflect on which one you identify with the most.

If you have not yet discovered your Instinctual Stack, we offer a test that can help you do so. The Instinctual Variant

Questionnaire (IVQ v2.0) will help you understand the role that all three Instincts play in your life. Once you have discovered your Instinctual Stack, you can understand your Enneagram type with even more depth and clarity.

Personality Type ONE: **The Reformer**

The Rational, Idealistic Type:

Principled, Purposeful, Self-Controlled, and Perfectionistic

Generally, Ones are conscientious, sensible, responsible, idealistic, ethical, serious, self-disciplined, orderly, and feel personally obligated to improve themselves and their world.

Ones get into conflicts by being opinionated, impatient, irritable, rigid, perfectionistic, critical (and self-critical), sarcastic, and judgmental.

At their best, Ones are tolerant, accepting, discerning, wise, humane, prudent, principled, fair, and able to delay rewards for a higher good.

Recognizing Ones

Type One exemplifies the desire to be good, to live up to the highest ethical standards, and to effect positive changes in the world. While a number of types care about achieving goals, Ones are particularly aware of how they achieve their goals. Were they honorable? Did they use their resources wisely? Were they fair and truthful? Ones are people of high standards and they expect themselves and others to live by those standards as much as possible. They tend to see things in terms of long-range objectives, and they can be aware of how current actions might affect future situations. For example, Ones are often in the forefront of battles to improve environmental standards or to make people aware of healthier lifestyle choices.

Most Ones report feeling a powerful sense of mission, a deep feeling of purpose that they remember from their early childhood. They sense that they are here for a reason and, unlike some other types, they have a fairly clear idea of what that reason is. This sense of mission impels Ones to rise to their highest standards, to make personal sacrifices, and to evaluate themselves regularly to see if they are falling short of their ideals. They feel that they must live a balanced, sensible life in order to have the clarity and inner resources necessary to fulfill their purpose.

Ones also have deep convictions about right and wrong, what is just and unjust. They are often dedicated to reform and social causes since they feel personally obligated to improve the world and leave it a better place. They put themselves on the line for their values and ethical convictions—if it means risking their jobs, their fortunes, or even their lives. Ones are convinced that there are indeed some truths—some values—that are worth both living and dying for. To accomplish their missions, Ones maintain self-discipline and do their best to practice "moderation in all things."

While Ones focus their attention on serious life issues, their high standards can also be directed to less significant matters— although they may seem equally important to Ones at the time. They can become extremely upset, for instance, if their spouse or one of their children fails to clean up after themselves adequately after using the bathroom sink. Ones are nothing if not thorough and well organized. Some Ones express this as an extraordinary concern with "neatness," the kind of people whose socks and underwear are folded neatly, whose file folders are labeled and filed alphabetically, and whose pencils are all sharpened. Other Ones focus their perfectionism in other areas, such as punctuality, ethical standards, political or religious ideals, office protocols, or uncovering misdeeds and untruths.

While Ones tend to see themselves as people of logic and reason, they are often driven by strong feelings and impulses— usually experienced as personal convictions. Because they so strongly feel that they must accomplish their life mission, they conclude that they must be serious and determined and must not waste time. They can become very strict with themselves, feeling they must always be working toward their ideals, "making progress," and pointing out how things could be improved. They are extremely conscientious about how they use their time and resources. Under pressure, time becomes a major interpersonal issue for Ones—they insist that they and others be punctual, efficient, and particular about details. They make lists, organize things, and constantly prioritize their activities. Their sense of obligation, however, can make them feel heavier and more burdened. Consequently, they begin to be afraid of making a mistake because they want everything to be consistent with their strict standards. At such times, others can perceive them as overly rigid and perfectionistic.

In brief, Ones want to be right, to strive higher and improve everything, to be consistent with their ideals, to justify themselves, and to be beyond criticism so as not to be condemned by anyone. Ones do not want to be proven wrong, to make mistakes, to allow sloppiness, to be with people they perceive as lazy or not serious, to be in chaos or in situations that seem out of control, or to be embarrassed by emotional display.

Their Hidden Side

Ones appear well balanced and sure of themselves, but they can suffer from extreme self-criticism, feeling that they are never able to measure up to their Olympian standards.

Similarly, they can feel lonely and alienated from others, seeing themselves as the only responsible adult around. At such times they feel burdened by their responsibilities and by the sense that others will not do as thorough a job as they will. If these feelings intensify, Ones can become harsh with themselves and others, and prey to hidden depression. They may attempt to maintain an outer attitude of self-control and reserve while inwardly feeling anguished and alienated. As they become more isolated, their self-criticism can become crueler and more irrational. Few casual observers would suspect how much they are suffering from the relentless attacks of their Inner Critic (superego).

Relationship Issues

Ones take their relationships and all of their responsibilities in relationships very seriously.

They are firmly committed to the people whom they love, and they are willing to make great personal sacrifices for the well-being of their intimates. As with other areas of life, Ones are idealistic and hold high standards for their relationships—it is important to them to have a partnership that is based on shared values and beliefs. When Ones get more stuck in their fixation, the following areas can create problems:

Holding the partner to strict standards that the partner does not wholeheartedly share.

Having difficulty finding a partner because of unrealistic standards—finding that no one "measures up."

Becoming moody, depressed, and uncommunicative because of repressed anger.

Not allowing enough "play time" in the relationship—feeling that all spare time must be used for serious purposes (yard work, checking finances, reading "educational" or "meaningful" books, attending meetings or lectures, discussing political issues, etc.).

Having issues with criticism: fearing criticism from their partner and also becoming critical of the partner—nitpicking, scolding, and correcting.

Type Compatibility

To learn more about compatibility issues and relationships with other types, see the Enneagram Type Combinations.

The Passion: Anger or Resentment

Feelings of obligation and of having higher standards than those around them leave Ones in a state of constant irritation with themselves, others, and the world. Nothing ever quite attains the ideal; nothing comes up to their exacting standards, leaving them feeling disappointed, frustrated, and resentful. But because such feelings conflict with their self-image of being rational and in control of themselves, they attempt to suppress their anger, unwittingly perpetuating it in the process. They become very inhibited, feeling that they must constantly hold their angry feelings and impulses in check. Ones may also hold their anger in their bodies, and they can become extremely tense and rigid with the effort to control themselves.

At Their Best

Healthy Ones are guided by their consciences and concerned with maintaining ethical standards, but they are also flexible and gentle about applying their principles—both with themselves and with others. They are truthful and reasonable—the kind of person others turn to for direction and clear feedback. They have a strong sense of morality, but they temper this with a deep love and respect for the dignity of their fellow human beings.

They strive to be impartial, fair, and objective, and they are willing to sublimate their desires and immediate gratification for "the greater good," or a higher principle.

Healthy Ones are motivated to "do the right thing" themselves and are not necessarily trying to fix anyone else. Even so, their personal integrity allows them to teach others by example. They can be quite eloquent and effective at conveying the truth and wisdom of their perspective.

They stand for quality and desire excellence in all things. Their commitment to the highest principles can be profoundly moving to others, reminding others of the values they most deeply cherish.

At their very best, high-functioning Ones embody true wisdom, especially in being able to discern appropriate and compassionate action. They radiate nobility and inspire others to remember to live according to the highest values. At the same time, they are gentle and humane: average Ones often feel disappointed with their fellow human beings, but healthy Ones feel a profound connection and kinship with everyone they encounter, giving them an abiding patience and affection for all humanity.

Personality Dynamics & Variations

Learn more about the Directions of Integration (Security) and Disintegration (Stress).

Under Stress (One goes to average Four)

Ones begin to feel alienated and moody when they sense that others do not take them or their values seriously. They feel obligated to do the work they believe others will not do—or will not do as well—and they become more resentful. They feel misunderstood by their peers and often withdraw from others to sort out their feelings, much like average-to unhealthy Fours. Similarly, Ones under prolonged stress can become disillusioned with themselves and their lot in life. Over time, they can become depressed and isolated, often turning to self-indulgent behavior in an attempt to feel better. They allow themselves various "escape hatches"— indulgences that go against their expressed values in some way. For instance, a One who is scrupulously observing rigorous health regimens and diets might start treating herself to ice cream sodas or chocolate bars. Guilt usually follows, leaving her more depressed and critical of herself.

Security (One goes to average Seven)

Ones become more playful and uninhibited in the company of people with whom they feel safe. It is as though a secure environment gives Ones permission to let their "silly side" out, along with the ability to express a more complete range of their emotions... They can be funny, talkative, tell jokes and long stories and can lead others into adventures of various kinds. They can also be boldly outspoken, impulsive, and "naughty" when they feel they can get away with it. They can also allow some of their needs to surface and become demanding, selfish, and greedy after the manner of a low-average Seven. Under stress, they may inadvertently look for distractions and begin to scatter their focus and their energies, as if to prevent becoming overwhelmed by the pressures they feel both from the obligations they have taken on and from their superego.

Integration (One goes to healthy Seven)

As Ones work through the basic issues of their type, they become less strict with themselves and begin to enjoy a greater freedom, lightness, and spontaneity, like healthy Sevens. Instead of feeling that everything is a personal obligation, they begin to experience choice, freedom, abundance, and joy. Whatever they do will be good and worthwhile, and they begin to live by the maxim, "Whatever is worth doing is worth doing badly." They let themselves off the hook of their strident superegos and begin to recognize what they want rather than what they "must" or "should" do. Integrating Ones can more easily access their curiosity and intelligence—their minds are open to many new possibilities. Their lighter approach helps other people hear their views and allows Ones to feel much closer to their fellow human beings. Rather than feeling resentful and obligated, they are filled with gratitude and a deep acceptance of themselves and others.

The Levels of Development

Learn more about the nine Levels of Development.

Healthy Levels

Level 1 (At Their Best): Become extraordinarily wise and discerning. By accepting what is, they become transcendentally realistic, knowing the best action to take in each moment. Humane, inspiring, and hopeful: the truth will be heard.

Level 2: Conscientious with strong personal convictions: they have an intense sense of right and wrong, personal religious and moral values. Wish to be rational, reasonable, self-disciplined, mature, moderate in all things.

Level 3: Extremely principled, always want to be fair, objective, and ethical: truth and justice primary values. Sense of responsibility, personal integrity, and of having a higher purpose often make them teachers and witnesses to the truth.

Average Levels

Level 4: Dissatisfied with reality, they become high-minded idealists, feeling that it is up to them to improve everything: crusaders, advocates, critics. Into "causes" and explaining to others how things "ought" to be.

Level 5: Afraid of making a mistake: everything must be consistent with their ideals.

Become orderly and well-organized, but impersonal, puritanical, emotionally constricted, rigidly keeping their feelings

and impulses in check. Often workaholics—
"anal compulsive," punctual, pedantic, and
fastidious.

Level 6: Highly critical both of self and
others: picky, judgmental, perfectionistic.
Very opinionated about everything:
correcting people and badgering them to
"do the right thing"—as they see it.
Impatient, never satisfied with anything
unless it is done according to their
prescriptions. Moralizing, scolding,
abrasive, and indignantly angry.

Unhealthy Levels

Level 7: Can be highly dogmatic, self-
righteous, intolerant, and inflexible. Begin
dealing in absolutes: they alone know "The
Truth." Everyone else is wrong: very severe
in judgments, while rationalizing own
actions.

Level 8: Become obsessive about
imperfection and the wrongdoing of

others, although they may fall into contradictory actions, hypocritically doing the opposite of what they preach.

Level 9: Become condemnatory toward others, punitive and cruel to rid themselves of wrongdoers. Severe depressions, nervous breakdowns, and suicide attempts are likely.

Generally, corresponds to the Obsessive-Compulsive and Depressive personality disorders.

Personal Growth Recommendations for Type Ones

Ones grow by recognizing that others do take things seriously too, but that their approach to problems or tasks might be different. As they become more centered in themselves, they become not only respectful of others' views, but curious about them.

They understand that their own wisdom can only be enriched by taking other perspectives into account. Ones also grow by playing—by finding areas of their lives that are lighter, freer, and that offer opportunities for spontaneous creativity. Most Ones have a great sense of humor, and the more they allow themselves to entertain and enjoy others, the better for everyone involved. Basically, Ones grow proportionately to the extent that they can accept reality with all of its apparent "imperfections." This, of course, especially applies to themselves. By accepting what is, and working with reality rather than judging it, they become transcendentally realistic, knowing the best action to take in each moment.

Learn to relax. Take some time for yourself, without feeling that everything is up to you or that what you do not accomplish will result in chaos and disaster. Mercifully, the salvation of the world does not depend on you alone, even though you may sometimes feel it does.

You have a lot to teach others and are probably a good teacher, but do not expect others to change immediately. What is obvious to you may not be as obvious to them, especially if they are not used to being as self-disciplined and objective about themselves as you are about yourself. Many people may also want to do what is right and may agree with you in principle but for various reasons simply cannot change right away. The fact that others do not change immediately according to your prescriptions does not mean that they will not change sometime in the future.

Your words and above all, your example may do more good than you realize, although they may take longer than you expect. So have patience.

It is easy for you to work yourself up into a lather about the wrongdoings of others.

And it may sometimes be true that they are wrong. But what is it to you? Your irritation with them will do nothing to help them see another way of being. Similarly, beware of your constant irritation with your own "shortcomings." Does your own harsh self-criticism really help you to improve? Or does it simply make you tense, nervous, and self-doubting? Learn to recognize the attacks of your superego and how they undermine you rather than helping you.

It is important for you to get in touch with your feelings, particularly your unconscious impulses. You may find that you are uneasy with your emotions and your sexual and aggressive impulses—in short, with the messy human things that make us human. It might be beneficial to keep a journal or to get into some kind of group therapy or other group work both to develop your emotions and to see that others will not condemn you for having human needs and limitations.

Your Achilles' heel is your self-righteous anger. You get angry easily and are offended by what seems to you to be the perverse refusal of others to do the right thing—as you have defined it. Try to step back and see that your anger alienates people so that they cannot hear many of the good things you have to say. Further, your own repressed anger may well be giving you an ulcer or high blood pressure and is a harbinger of worse things to come.

Examples

Confucius, Plato, Salahuddin Ayyubi, Joan of Arc, Sir Thomas More, Mahatma Gandhi, Pope John Paul II, Nelson Mandela, Margaret Thatcher, Prince Charles, Kate Middleton, Duchess of Cambridge, Jimmy Carter, Michelle Obama, Al Gore, Hilary

Clinton, Rudy Giuliani, Elliot Spitzer, Justice
Sandra Day O'Connor, Osama bin Laden,
George Bernard Shaw, Thoreau, Dr. Jack
Kevorkian, Anita Roddick (The Body Shop),
Martha Stewart, Chef Thomas Keller,
Michio Kushi (macrobiotics), George
Harrison, Joan Baez, Celine Dion, Ralph
Nader, Noam Chomsky, Bill Moyers,
George F. Will, William F. Buckley, Keith
Olbermann, Jerry Seinfeld, Bill Maher, Tina
Fey, Katherine Hepburn, Maggie Smith,
Emma Thompson, Julie Andrews, Vanessa
Redgrave, Jane Fonda, Meryl Streep,
Harrison Ford, Helen Hunt, Captain "Sully"
Sullenberger, "Mary Poppins," "Mr.
Spock," SNL's "The Church Lady"

Personality Type FOUR: The **Individualist**

The Sensitive, Introspective Type:

Expressive, Dramatic, Self-Absorbed, and
Temperamental

Generally, Fours are intuitive, sensitive, impressionable, quiet, introspective, passionate, romantic, elegant, witty, imaginative, and self-expressive.

Fours get into conflicts by being moody, emotionally demanding, self-absorbed, withholding, temperamental, dramatic, pretentious, and self-indulgent.

At their best, Fours are creative, inspired, honest with themselves, emotionally strong, humane, self-aware, discrete, and self-renewing.

Recognizing Fours

Type Four exemplifies the desire to be ourselves, to be known for who we are, and to know the depths of our hearts. Of all the types, Fours are the most aware of their own emotional states. They notice when they feel upset, anxious, attracted to another person, or some other, more subtle combination of feelings. They pay attention to their different changing emotions and try to determine what their feelings are telling them about themselves, others, and their world. When Fours are more in balance, their exquisite attunement to their inner states enables them to discover deep truths about human nature, to bear compassionate witness to the suffering of others, or to be profoundly honest with themselves about their own motives. When they are less balanced, they can become lost in their feelings, preoccupied with emotional reactions, memories, and fantasies, both negative and positive.

Fours are nothing if not subtle and expressive, and they are able to put words to feelings and states that others may recognize but could not have expressed as eloquently. ("That poem exactly captures how I felt about leaving home.") By being emotionally honest, and by taking time to see what they really feel about things, they encourage others to look more deeply into themselves.

Fours are also people who care a great deal about beauty and taste. Many Fours, for instance, are involved in artistic pursuits. Even if they are not artistically creative themselves, Fours seek out art, poetry, music, and other expressions that they find beautiful, because they feel these things reveal something true about themselves and about human nature. Fours often dress in ways that accentuate their own sense of personal style but also in ways that symbolically let others know how they are feeling (dressing entirely in black or in shades of violet, for instance). Similarly, they typically decorate their homes with objects and colors that evoke a strong sense of image and mood and reflect personal feelings and associations.

Above all, Fours want to distinguish themselves from others—they want to feel that their taste, their self-expression, and their emotional depth are unique. Thus, they tend to emphasize all of the ways in which they are unlike other people— especially their own family. They deeply want to know who they are and that who they are is special in some way. Being complimented or told that they are loved is nice, of course, but what Fours really want is for others to recognize and appreciate the pattern of qualities that is unique to them—that they are not generic.

Because of their powerful need to see themselves as different from others, Fours often end up feeling alone and misunderstood. They become creative "outsiders," and they are proud of it. If they are working in a regular nine-to-five job, they will find ways to put their unique stamp on their work. This can run the gamut from finding their own way of presenting reports to having a recognizable design style to decorating their office in a way that reflects their tastes and feelings. They may run their own company (as long as there's a creative component to their work and it's emotionally satisfying), or they may be in a profession that makes use of their personal touch, such as a clothing designer, or counselor, or a therapist of some kind. Fours are often professional artists, writers, or teachers. Above all, Fours want their life to be a work of art. They want to achieve something beautiful despite the loneliness, suffering, and self-doubt they have so often felt.

Unfortunately, the Four's need to be different can also lead to alienation and a tendency to become engrossed in feelings of loss, sadness, and melancholy. All nine types can feel sad, lonely, or depressed, but Fours feel this way frequently—even when there is nothing in their current lives to cause such feelings. They often become convinced that these painful feelings are more real and authentic when compared to more passing feelings of happiness or enthusiasm. Indeed, Fours begin to feel that they are being the most real, most honest people because they are focusing on disappointment and sadness.

Ultimately, this can lead them to foster and prolong these painful feelings in themselves. In brief, Fours want to express themselves and their individuality, to create and surround themselves with beauty, to maintain certain moods and feelings, to withdraw and protect their vulnerabilities, to take care of emotional needs before attending to anything else, and to attract a "rescuer" who will understand them. Fours do not want to restrain or lose touch with their emotions, to feel ordinary, to have their individuality unrecognized, to have their taste questioned, to be required at social settings, to follow impersonal rules and procedures, to spend time with people they perceive as lacking taste or emotional depth.

Their Hidden Side

On the surface, Fours can seem to suffer from chronic self-doubt and extreme sensitivity to others' reactions to them. But part of the reason for this is that Fours often hold a secret, inner image of who they feel they could be. They have an idea of the sort of person they would like to become, the kind of person who would be fantastically talented, socially adept, and intensely desired. In short, Fours come to believe that if they were somehow different from who they are, they would be seen and loved. Unfortunately, they constantly compare themselves negatively to this idealized secret self—their 'fantasy self." This makes it very difficult for Fours to appreciate many of their genuine positive qualities because they are never as wonderful as the fantasy. Much of the growth for type Four involves letting go of this idealized secret self so that they can see and appreciate who they actually are.

Relationship Issues

As the romantics of the Enneagram, Fours focus a great deal of their time and attention on their relationships. High-functioning Fours are sensitive to others—especially to others' feelings—and enjoy any kind of authentic personal sharing. They are excellent listeners and give their full attention when someone they care about is trying to express herself. Unfortunately, Fours also tend to get caught up in their own emotional reactions and dramas. When this happens, they have difficulty seeing others or hearing them objectively. Their strong emotional reactions can make it difficult for them to sustain interpersonal connections. Fours tend to have the following issues in relationships:

Becoming self-absorbed and uninterested in others' feelings or problems due to feeling overwhelmed by their own feelings.

Idealizing potential partners, then feeling disappointed once they get to know them—often devaluing and rejecting them.

Placing great expectations on the partner for nurturing and support.

Being moody and temperamental—making others "walk on eggshells."

Withholding attention and affection to punish the other.

Imagining that others have worse opinions of them than they do—being touchy and hypersensitive to slights.

Type Compatibility

To learn more about compatibility issues and relationships with other types, see the Enneagram Type Combinations.

The Passion: Envy

At some level, Fours believe that they are missing something that other people seem to have. They feel that something is wrong with them or with their relationships, and they start to be acutely aware of what is not working in their lives. Naturally, given this frame of mind, it is difficult for Fours to feel good about themselves or to appreciate the good things in their world.

Fours rightly perceive that there is something inadequate or incomplete about the ego self, but they incorrectly assume that they alone suffer from this problem. Fours then get in the habit of comparing themselves to others, concluding that they have somehow gotten "the short end of the stick." Fours feel that they have been singled out by fate for bad treatment, bad luck, unsatisfying relationships, bad parenting, and broken dreams. It comes as something of a shock to many Fours to discover that other people have suffered as much as or even more than they have. This doesn't mean that Fours haven't suffered or that their painful pasts are inconsequential. But Fours need to see how they perpetuate their own suffering by continually focusing on old wounds rather than truly processing those hurts and letting go of them in a way that would allow them to heal.

At Their Best

Healthy Fours strive to be true to themselves. They are emotionally honest and aren't afraid to reveal themselves to others, "warts and all." They combine self-awareness and introspection with great emotional strength and endurance. They bring a heightened sensitivity to their experiences and are able to share with others the subtleties of their inner world. This invites others to do the same. They are highly intuitive and creative and add a personal, human touch to whatever they are involved with. They treat others with gentleness, tact, and discretion. They can be wonderfully expressive with an ironic, witty view of life and themselves, often finding humor in their own foibles and contradictions.

They bring a sense of beauty, refinement, and emotional richness into other people's lives.

Thus, high-functioning Fours are profoundly creative, expressing the personal and the universal, possibly through art but also in their daily lives. They are in touch with the everchanging nature of reality and are inspired by it. High-functioning Fours are able to renew and regenerate themselves again and again, transforming even their most painful experiences into something beautiful and meaningful that others can benefit from as well.

They have a deep sense of "allowing," and they are able to hold even the most painful feelings with compassion and sensitivity—whether their own or someone else's.

Personality Dynamics & Variations

Learn more about the Directions of Integration (Security) and Disintegration (Stress).

Under Stress (Four Goes to Average Two)

Fours attempt to defend their hurt feelings (and gain attention) by withdrawing from people and withholding their own affection and attention. They may recognize on some level, however, that their emotional storminess and withdrawals are driving away the people who are most supportive of them. Then Fours go out of their way to reestablish their connections and reassure themselves that their relationship is still on solid ground.

But because they are reacting out of stress, Fours may overcompensate by trying to win others over, by doing favors, or, more darkly, by manipulation and creating dependencies, all in the manner of average-to-unhealthy Twos. To do this, they keep talking about the state of the relationship with the other person and try to make themselves more needed.

Favors, help, and reminding others of their support are part of the picture. Troubled Fours also become more possessive of loved ones, not wanting to let them out of their sight for long, like lower-functioning Twos.

Security: (Four Goes to Average One)

With trusted intimates, or in situations in which Fours feel sure of themselves, they may risk being more openly controlling and critical of others. Their frustration with others and feeling of disappointment in how others are behaving (especially toward them) finally erupts. Fours can become impatient and critical, demanding that people meet their exacting standards, constantly pointing out how others have made errors. Nothing about the other person (whom they may have idealized and regarded as their longed for "rescuer") now satisfies them or gives them much hope or pleasure. Everything about the person and their situation becomes irritating and annoying and they can't seem to get the other person's faults out of their mind. Fours in this state may also compensate for their ragged emotions by driving themselves excessively, feeling that they are lazy and unproductive if they are not constantly working and improving.

Integration (Four Goes to Healthy One)

As Fours become more aware of their tendency to brood and to fantasize about their many hurts and disappointments, they also become aware of the cost to themselves of this way of being. As they relax and accept themselves more deeply, they gradually become free of their

constant emotional turbulence and their
need to maintain emotional crises or to
indulge themselves as a consolation prize
for not fulfilling their potential.

Gradually and naturally, they become more
objective, grounded, and practical, like
healthy Ones. They also become more
realistic and able to operate in the real
world.

Without imposing harsh disciplines or
expectations on themselves, integrating
Fours want to become involved in matters
beyond themselves, such as in community
work, politics, the environment, or in other
worthwhile ways to engage their minds
and hearts. On some level, they choose no
longer to indulge themselves but to live
within the constraints of reality. When
they do so, they find the payoffs and the
pleasures—and their creativity—are
deeper and much more fulfilling.

The Levels of Development

Learn more about the nine Levels of Development.

Healthy Levels

Level 1 (At Their Best): Profoundly creative, expressing the personal and the universal, possibly in a work of art. Inspired, self-renewing and regenerating: able to transform all their experiences into something valuable: self-creative.

Level 2: Self-aware, introspective, on the "search for self," aware of feelings and inner impulses. Sensitive and intuitive both to self and others: gentle, tactful, compassionate.

Level 3: Highly personal, individualistic, "true to self." Self-revealing, emotionally honest, humane. Ironic view of self and life: can be serious and funny, vulnerable and emotionally strong.

Average Levels

Level 4: Take an artistic, romantic orientation to life, creating a beautiful, aesthetic environment to cultivate and prolong personal feelings. Heighten reality through fantasy, passionate feelings, and the imagination.

Level 5: To stay in touch with feelings, they interiorize everything, taking everything personally, but become self-absorbed and introverted, moody and hypersensitive, shy and self-conscious, unable to be spontaneous or to "get out of themselves." Stay withdrawn to protect their self-image and to buy time to sort out feelings.

Level 6: Gradually think that they are different from others, and feel that they are exempt from living as everyone else does. They become melancholy dreamers, disdainful, decadent, and sensual, living in a fantasy world. Self-pity and envy of others leads to self-indulgence, and to becoming increasingly impractical, unproductive, effete, and precious.

Unhealthy Levels

Level 7: When dreams fail, become self-inhibiting and angry at self, depressed and alienated from self and others, blocked and emotionally paralyzed. Ashamed of self, fatigued and unable to function.

Level 8: Tormented by delusional self-contempt, self-reproaches, self-hatred, and morbid thoughts: everything is a source of torment. Blaming others, they drive away anyone who tries to help them.

Level 9: Despairing, feel hopeless and become self-destructive, possibly abusing alcohol or drugs to escape. In the extreme: emotional breakdown or suicide is likely. Generally corresponds to the Avoidant, Depressive, and Narcissistic personality disorders.

Personal Growth Recommendations for Type Fours

Fours grow by recognizing that while the hurts and losses of the past were real enough, there is no need to keep revisiting them in the imagination. On the contrary, doing so keeps drawing them out of the richness and depth of the present moment—the one time and place in which their real feelings and their true identity can be found. Fours need to see how working up their feelings actually moves them further away from their most authentic self and their truest self-expression.

Do not pay so much attention to your feelings; they are not a true source of support for you, as you probably already know. Remember this advice: "From our present perspective, we can also see that one of the most important mistakes Fours make is to equate themselves with their feelings. The fallacy is that to understand themselves they must understand their feelings, particularly their negative ones, before acting. Fours do not see that the self is not the same as its feelings or that the presence of negative feelings does not preclude the presence of good in themselves" (Personality Types, p. 172). Always remember that your feelings are telling you something about yourself as you are at this particular moment, not necessarily more than that.

Avoid putting off things until you are "in the right mood." Commit yourself to productive, meaningful work that will contribute to your good and that of others, no matter how small the contribution may be. Working consistently in the real world will create a context in which you can discover yourself and your talents. (Actually, you are happiest when you are working—that is, activating your potentials and realizing yourself. You will not "find yourself" in a vacuum or while waiting for inspiration to strike, so connect—and stay connected—with the real world.

Self-esteem and self-confidence will develop only from having positive experiences, whether or not you believe that you are ready to have them. Therefore, put yourself in the way of good. You may never feel that you are ready to take on a challenge of some sort, that you always need more time. (Fours typically never feel that they are sufficiently "together," but they must nevertheless have the courage to stop putting off their lives.) Even if you start small, commit yourself to doing something that will bring out the best in you.

A wholesome self-discipline takes many forms, from sleeping regular hours to working regularly to exercising regularly, and has a cumulative, strengthening effect.

Since it comes from yourself, a healthy self-discipline is not contrary to your freedom or individuality. On the other hand, sensuality, excessive sexual experiences, alcohol, drugs, sleep, or fantasizing have a debilitating effect on you, as you already know. Therefore, practice healthy self-discipline and stay with it.

Avoid lengthy conversations in your imagination, particularly if they are negative, resentful, or even excessively romantic. These conversations are essentially unreal and at best only rehearsals for action—although, as you know, you almost never say or do what you imagine you will. Instead of spending time imagining your life and relationships, begin to live them.

Examples

Rumi, Frédéric Chopin, Pyotr I. Tchaikovsky, Gustav Mahler, Jackie

Kennedy Onassis, Edgar Allen Poe, Yukio Mishima, Virginia Woolf, Anne Frank , Karen Blixen / Isak Dinesen, Anaîs Nin, Tennessee Williams, J.D. Salinger, Anne Rice, Frida Kahlo, Diane Arbus, Martha Graham, Rudolf Nureyev, Cindy Sherman, Hank Williams, Billie Holiday, Judy Garland, Maria Callas, Miles Davis, Keith Jarrett, Joni Mitchell, Bob Dylan, Paul Simon, Leonard Cohen, Yusuf Islam (Cat Stevens), Ferron, Cher, Stevie Nicks, Annie Lennox, Prince, Sarah McLachlan, Alanis Morrisette, Feist, Florence (+ the Machine) Welch, Amy Winehouse, Ingmar Bergman, Lars von Trier, Marlon Brando, Jeremy Irons, Angelina Jolie, Winona Ryder, Kate Winslet, Nicolas Cage, Johnny Depp, Tattoo Artist Kat Von D., Magician Criss Angel, Streetcar Named Desire's "Blanche duBois".

Personality Type EIGHT: **The Challenger**

The Powerful, Dominating Type:

Self-Confident, Decisive, Willful, and Confrontational

Generally, Eights are strong, assertive, resourceful, independent, determined, action-oriented, pragmatic, competitive, straight-talking, shrewd, and insistent.

Eights get into conflicts by being blunt, willful, domineering, forceful, defiant, confrontational, bad-tempered, rageful, cynical, and vengeful.

At their best, Eights are honorable, heroic, empowering, generous, gentle, constructive, initiating, decisive, and inspiring.

Recognizing Eights

Type Eight exemplifies the desire to be independent and to take care of oneself. Eights are assertive and passionate about life, meeting it head on with self-confidence and strength. They have learned to stand up for themselves and have a resourceful, "can-do" attitude. They are determined to be self-reliant and free to pursue their own destiny.

Thus, Eights are natural leaders: honorable, authoritative, and decisive, with a solid, commanding presence. They take initiative and make things happen, protecting and providing for the people in their lives while empowering others to stand on their own.

They embody solidity and courage, using their talents and vision to construct a better world for everyone depending on the range of the influence.

Most of all, Eights are people of vision and action. They can take what looks like a useless, broken-down shell of a building and turn it into a beautiful home or office or hospital. Likewise, they see possibilities in people, and they like to offer incentives and challenges to bring out people's strengths. Eights agree with the saying "Give a person a fish and they eat for a day. But teach them how to fish, and they can feed themselves for life." Eights know this is true because they have often taught themselves "how to fish."

They are self-starters and enjoy constructive activity—building up themselves, others, and their world.

Eights occasionally take on big challenges to see if they can pull off the impossible or turn a hopeless cause into a great success. But they generally do not do so unless they are fairly sure that the odds are on their side and that they will have the resources to pull off a "long shot" and make it look easy. Others look to them in times of crisis because they know that Eights are willing to make tough decisions and to take the heat if things go wrong.

Honor is also important to Eights because their word is their bond. When they say "You have my word on this," they mean it. Eights want to be respected, and healthy

Eights also extend respect to others, affirming the dignity of whomever they encounter. They react strongly when they see someone being taken advantage of or treated in a demeaning or degrading manner. They will step in and stop a fight to protect the weak or disadvantaged or to "even the score" for those whom they feel have been wronged. Similarly, Eights would not hesitate to give up their seat on the train to an old or sick person, but they would have to be dragged away bodily if anyone tried to make them give it up without their consent.

Nothing much about Eights is half-hearted. They have powerful feelings and drives and often have a major impact on the people around them—for good or for ill. Eights are more intense and direct than most, and they expect others to meet these qualities as well.

Indirectness of any kind drives them crazy, and they will keep pushing and raising their energy level until they feel that others have sufficiently responded to them.

Many Eights have some kind of a dream for themselves and their "inner circle," and being the practical-minded people that they are, this often involves money-making projects, business ventures, philanthropy, and the like. They may start and run their own business or set someone else up in a situation or simply play the state lottery on a regular basis.

Not all Eights have a lot of money, but most are looking for some kind of "big break" that would give them the independence, respect, and sense of power that they typically want.

They can also be highly competitive, enjoying the challenges and risks of their own enterprises. They are hard-working and pragmatic—"rugged individualists," and **wheeler-dealers** who are always thinking of a new angle and constantly have a new project underway.

Less healthy Eights can become extremely controlling, self-important, confrontational, and highly territorial. They may respond to others by swaggering and being willful, bluffing and "throwing their weight around" in various ways. Average Eights are full of bluster and bravado to get people to fall in line with their plans, desires, and if they encounter resistance, they will try to control and dominate people more openly and aggressively.

Whether they are running a multinational corporation or a family of two, they want it understood that they are firmly and clearly in charge.

In brief, Eights want to be self-reliant, to prove their strength and independence, to be important in their world, to have an impact on their environment, to have the unquestioned loyalty of their inner circle, and to stay in control of their situation. Eights do not want to feel weak or vulnerable, to feel out of control, to be dependent on others, to have their decisions or authority questioned, to lose others' backing, or to be surprised by others' unexpected actions.

Their Hidden Side

Eights present a tough, independent image to the world, but under their bravado and layers of armor, there is vulnerability and fear. Eights are affected by the reactions of those closest to them far more than they want to let on. They often expect that others will dislike or reject them, and so they are profoundly touched, even sentimental, when they feel that someone they care about truly understands them and loves them. Eights may learn to harden themselves against wanting or expecting tenderness, but they are never entirely successful. No matter how tough, even belligerent, they may become, their desire for nurturance and connection can never be put entirely out of consciousness.

Relationship Issues

Eights are often sought out as partners because they appear so confident, capable, and strong. Others are reassured by their solidity and feel that the Eight will offer protection and stability in the relationship. (When Eights are healthy, this is true.) Eights also exude a great deal of charisma—they have tremendous instinctual energy and many people feel attracted to their intensity. However, other people may be frightened by the same qualities in Eights, and when Eights assert their energy too forcefully, they often create problems in their relationships. Some of their main trouble spots include the following:

Becoming self-absorbed and uninterested in others' feelings or problems due to feeling overwhelmed by their own feelings.

Overreacting to perceived rejection by withdrawing or losing their temper.

Pushing others to get a more "genuine" response.

Becoming remote and emotionally unavailable when troubled.

Becoming possessive and jealous of the partner.

Seeing the other as an inferior to be shaped and directed; not respecting the partner as an equal.

Acting out difficult psychological issues in rages, binges, or acts of revenge.

Type Compatibility

To learn more about compatibility issues and relationships with other types, see the Enneagram Type Combinations.

The Passion: Lust

Eights want to feel intensely alive: they love the sense of immediacy they get from being engaged with life fully. They do not have much patience with lukewarm responses or halfhearted actions from others. But this desire to be vital and alive can easily deteriorate into a need to constantly push against the world—and especially other people. Eights get into the habit of exerting themselves and their influence, increasing the intensity of situations so that they will feel more real and alive. They become like a person aggressively trying to push a door open that opens inwardly. Unfortunately, this approach to life often overwhelms other people who then avoid the Eight, and it can lead to severe stress and even physical breakdown for the Eight herself.

At Their Best Healthy Eights combine their natural strength and energy with measured, insightful, decision-making, and a greater willingness to be emotionally open and available to others. They make loyal friends and will make any sacrifice necessary for the well-being of their loved ones. They feel no need to test their wills against others: they are so secure and grounded in themselves that there is no need to constantly assert themselves much less to control anyone else. Thus, they have greater inner peace themselves and can therefore be enormous sources of support and strength for others. Seeing that they can be a powerful source of blessings in others' lives fills Eights with a deep sense of fulfillment and a kind of benevolent pride in their ability to have a positive impact on the world and on others.

High-functioning Eights are truly heroic, mastering themselves and their passions.

They are big-hearted, merciful, and forbearing, carrying others with their strength. Courageous and strong, but also gentle and humble—willing to put themselves in jeopardy for the sake of justice and fairness. Very high-functioning Eights have the vision, compassion, and heart to be a tremendous influence for good in the world.

Personality Dynamics & Variations

Learn more about the Directions of Integration (Security) and Disintegration (Stress).

Under Stress (Eight Goes to Average Five)

Eights usually respond to stress by taking problems and challenges head on. They are bold and assertive in pushing for control and for accomplishing their vision, whatever it might be. But this approach can leave them feeling beleaguered and overwhelmed. When stress levels get too high, Eights may suddenly switch tactics and go into periods of retreat or even isolation, like average Fives. They pull back from the front lines to assess their situation, to strategize, and to see how they can regain control. They may become strangely quiet, secretive, and isolated as they privately explore ways to deal with their problems. Under longer periods of stress, they may also develop a cold, cynical attitude about themselves, other people, and life in general, in the manner of less healthy Fives.

Security (Eight Goes to Average Two)

Eights will sometimes turn toward people they trust to be reassured about the other person's need for them. They have an emotional, even sentimental side that they show only to people with whom they feel safe. They may appear tough and independent in public while privately doting on key people in their lives or, if they lack these, then on their pets. They may also attempt to get intimates to acknowledge their help and support or may want people to depend more completely on them, like average Twos. Hidden feelings of rejection can cause them to seek ways to hold on to those few people they feel close to, including manipulation and undermining the other. Like average Twos, they also become unwilling to acknowledge their real needs or feelings of hurt with people on whom they depend.

Integration (Eight Goes to Healthy Two)

As Eights begin to recognize their powerful emotional armoring and see how much it isolates them unnecessarily, they naturally become more emotionally expressive and generous, like high-functioning Twos. Underneath their drive for self-protection and independence, Eights have big hearts and generous impulses. Once they feel secure enough to let down their guards, they discover how much they care about people and how much they want to support others. In short, they want to be a source of good in the world and to express their love—and at Two, they do so. Since they remain Eights, their love is expressed in palpable ways that actually help and support people. It is a love free of sentiment, clinging, or hidden agenda, and through it, Eights find the sense of empowerment and dignity that they have been seeking.

The Levels of Development

Learn more about the nine Levels of Development.

Healthy Levels

Level 1 (At Their Best): Become self-restrained and magnanimous, merciful and forbearing, mastering self through their self-surrender to a higher authority.

Courageous, willing to put self in serious jeopardy to achieve their vision and have a lasting influence. May achieve true heroism and historical greatness.

Level 2: Self-assertive, self-confident, and strong: have learned to stand up for what they need and want. A resourceful, "can do" attitude and passionate inner drive.

Level 3: Decisive, authoritative, and commanding: the natural leader others look up to. Take initiative, make things happen: champion people, provider, protective, and honorable, carrying others with their strength.

Average Levels

Level 4: Self-sufficiency, financial independence, and having enough resources are important concerns: become enterprising, pragmatic, "rugged individualists," wheeler-dealers. Risk-taking, hardworking, denying own emotional needs.

Level 5: Begin to dominate their environment, including others: want to feel that others are behind them, supporting their efforts. Swaggering, boastful, forceful, and expansive: **the "boss"** whose word is law. Proud, egocentric, want to impose their will and vision on everything, not seeing others as equals or treating them with respect.

Level 6: Become highly combative and intimidating to get their way: confrontational, belligerent, creating adversarial relationships. Everything a test of wills, and they will not back down. Use threats and reprisals to get obedience from others, to keep others off balance and insecure. However, unjust treatment makes others fear and resent them, possibly also band together against them.

Unhealthy Levels

Level 7: Defying any attempt to control them, become completely ruthless, dictatorial, "might makes right." The criminal and outlaw, renegade, and con-artist. Hard-hearted, immoral and potentially violent.

Level 8: Develop delusional ideas about their power, invincibility, and ability to prevail: megalomania, feeling omnipotent, invulnerable. Recklessly over-extending self.

Level 9: If they get in danger, they may brutally destroy everything that has not conformed to their will rather than surrender to anyone else. Vengeful, barbaric, murderous. Sociopathic tendencies. Generally corresponds to the Antisocial Personality Disorder.

Personal Growth Recommendations for Type Eights

Eights grow by recognizing that the world is not a battleground to be approached as a gigantic test of wills. They do not have to see life as a "survival of the fittest," a titanic struggle that they must be constantly engaged in. They grow by recognizing that it is their attempt to defy the world and to force everything to bend to their will that is at the root of their problems. They realize that any real strength entails vulnerability and openness.

They also learn that allowing more openness enables others to get closer to them and to support them in tangible ways. Eights grow by recognizing that more can be accomplished through cooperation and partnership than they can do by themselves or by constantly struggling to impose their will on others.

It goes against the grain, but act with self-restraint. You show true power when you forbear from asserting your will with others, even when you could. Your real power lies in your ability to inspire and uplift people. You are at your best when you take charge and help everyone through a crisis. Few will take advantage of you when you are caring, and you will do more to secure the loyalty and devotion of others by showing the greatness of your heart than you ever could by displays of raw power.

It is difficult for Eights, but learn to yield to others, at least occasionally. Often, little is really at stake, and you can allow others to have their way without fear of sacrificing your power, or your real needs. The desire to dominate everyone all the time is a sign that your ego is beginning to inflate—a danger signal that more serious conflicts with others are inevitable.

Remember that the world is not against you. Many people in your life care about you and look up to you, but when you are in your fixation, you do not make this easy for them. Let in the affection that is available. Doing this will not make you weak, but will confirm the strength and support in yourself and your life. Also remember that by believing that others are against you and reacting against them, you tend to alienate them and confirm your own fears. Take stock of the people who truly are on your side, and let them know how important they are to you.

Eights typically want to be self-reliant and depend on no one. But, ironically, they depend on many people. For example, you may think that you are not dependent on your employees because they depend on you for their jobs. You could dismiss them at any time and hire other workers. Everyone is expendable in your little kingdom—except you. But the fact is that you are dependent on others to do their jobs too, especially if your business concerns grow beyond what you can manage alone. But if you alienate everyone associated with you, you will eventually be forced to employ the most obsequious and untrustworthy operatives. When you do, you will have reason to question their loyalty and to fear losing your position. The fact is that whether in your business world or your domestic life, yourself-sufficiency is largely an illusion.

Eights typically overvalue power. Having power, whether through wealth, position, or simple brute force, allows them to do whatever they want, to feel important, to be feared and obeyed. But those who are attracted to you because of your power do not love you for yourself, nor do you love or respect them. While this may be the Faustian bargain you have made, you will nevertheless have to pay the price that whatever power you accumulated will inevitably be at a cost you, physically and emotionally.

Examples

G.I. Gurdjieff, Richard Wagner, Franklin D. Roosevelt, Winston Churchill, Oskar Schindler, Fidel Castro, Martin Luther King, Jr., Lyndon Johnson, Mikhail Gorbachev, Golda Meir, Indira Gandhi, Saddam Hussein, Senator John McCain, Donald Trump, Pablo Picasso, Ernest Hemingway, Norman Mailer, Toni Morrison, Serena Williams, James Brown, Aretha Franklin, Keith Richards, Queen Latifah, Courtney Love, Jack Black, Chrissie Hynde, Pink, John Wayne, Frank Sinatra, Humphrey Bogart, Lauren Bacall, Bette Davis, Mae West, Sean Connery, Paul Newman, Clint Eastwood, Tommy Lee Jones, Jack Nicholson, Susan Sarandon, Russell Crowe, Sean Penn, Harvey Keitel, Matt Damon, Alec Baldwin, Roseanne Barr, Barbara Walters, Rosie

O'Donnell, "Dr. Phil" McGraw, "Tony Soprano".

Personality Type THREE: **The Achiever**

The Success-Oriented, Efficient Type:

Adaptive, Excelling, Driven, and Image-Conscious

Generally, Threes are effective, competent, adaptable, **goal oriented, ambitious, organized**, diplomatic, charming, into performance, and **image-conscious**.

Threes get into conflicts by being expedient, excessively driven, competitive, self-promoting, "appropriate" instead of sincere, boastful, and grandiose.

At their best, Threes are inner-directed, authentic, modest, admirable, well-adjusted, gracious, interested in others, and self-accepting.

Recognizing Threes

Type Three exemplifies the desire to be our best self, to develop all of our potentials, and to value ourselves and others.

Threes are the "stars" of the personality types—people of tremendous drive, ambition, and belief in themselves. Threes want to excel, to be the best at whatever they do, and they are willing to put in the effort it takes to do so. Threes can be found at the gym, taking classes at night, putting in extra hours at work, learning how to coordinate their best colors when they dress—basically doing what it takes to shine. While Threes are energetic and ambitious, they are also diplomatic—they want to be liked and esteemed by others. They strive to be presentable and appropriate, not wanting to come across in ways that would be disapproved of. They know how to put their best foot forward and present themselves in a way that highlights their energy and confidence.

Threes are, above all, goal-oriented. They get a particular objective in their sights and then actively engage in activities that will bring them closer to whatever they seek. They pursue their dreams tirelessly, and cannot understand why others are not similarly motivated. Thus, Threes also enjoy sharing self-development tips, explaining how to make money, lose weight, develop career skills, and so forth. They are hard workers, diligent and effective—and they like helping others to be that way, too.

To achieve their goals, Threes learn to be highly adaptable. They are able to change course when necessary and may even do so several times, including a change of career, if that is what it takes. They may try different approaches to problems until they find a formula that seems the most effective. Similarly, Threes quickly adapt to different social settings, always wanting to be appropriate and to exemplify the values of whatever group they are in. While their adaptability can be an enormous asset, it can also be overdone, leaving Threes unsure of who they are or what their own deepest values are.

In all of their dealings, Threes value efficiency and effectiveness, and they are often prized by businesses for these values. They are extremely goal-driven, and once they are given a task to perform, will do their best to make sure that it is done as quickly and efficiently as possible. The problem is that Threes can be efficient to a fault—becoming accomplishment machines, brushing their real feelings and needs aside to "get the job done." This way of living can leave Threes feeling empty and emotionally isolated, despite the successes they may be having.

Problem arise because Threes learned in childhood that they are only valuable for their accomplishments and self-presentation. They believe that they will only be loved if they become extraordinary in some field of endeavor. Thus, the pressure to be outstanding in whatever they do is intense and draining. Even if they are not working at a career and are primarily keeping a home, they will strive to have the most outstanding home in their neighborhood and to be "Super-Mom" or "Super-Dad." Threes find it difficult to stop or rest when they are caught up in their drive for success. They believe that to do so is to risk failure—and most Threes would rather die than fail and risk being humiliated. Their drive for success can also create conflicts with their personal or family life. Similarly, intimacy issues are not uncommon.

When Threes push themselves too hard and are unable to deliver everything that they would like to, they may resort to presenting successful images to others rather than letting people know their actual state or emotional condition. They attempt to convince others and themselves that they have no problems and that they are doing great, even though they may feel depressed or even burnt out. They believe that they can "fake it until they make it," but if Threes do not slow down to deal with their emotional problems, sooner or later, a crash is inevitable.

In brief, Threes want to feel valuable and worthwhile, to excel, to be affirmed, to be effective and efficient, to perform well, to be "the best," to have attention, to be admired, and to impress others. Threes do not want anything that looks like failure, to sit around "doing nothing," to be overshadowed by others, to look unprepared or awkward, to be average, to ask others for help or support, or to be caught in distortions of the truth.

Their Hidden Side

Beneath the surface, Threes have deep anxieties about their personal value. They feel that unless they maintain a certain position or image in life, they will be devalued, rejected, and tossed aside as worthless. Thus, they feel a constant inner pressure to "have it together," to not need much intimacy or personal support, and, above all, to constantly perform at maximum efficiency. Unless you knew a Three very well, you would never suspect the degree of emotional vulnerability and insecurity that they conceal beneath their smooth, efficient surface. The fact is that despite Threes' apparent social ease, there is great loneliness and a belief that they must not need help or support. As much as possible, Threes try to avoid their feelings of shame and isolation, but a large part of their growth entails allowing these feelings to arise and become integrated into their functioning self.

Relationship Issues

Threes often report that they feel confident in their ability to attract other people. They are usually charming and magnetic, and they know how to behave appropriately. Also, many Threes spend significant time and resources cultivating their personal presentation. They work at being in good physical condition and are often well-groomed. They want their partner to be proud of them and their accomplishments, so they often are drawn to people who they believe will appreciate them. The problem is that Threes fear that many parts of themselves may be less than outstanding or even unacceptable. Fears of potential rejection may prevent them from letting people get close to them. Significant relationship issues include the following:

Holding the partner to strict standards that the partner does not wholeheartedly share.

Presenting a favorable image that they later fear they will not be able to live up to.

Fearing that people only want them for their looks or abilities.

Not speaking up when they need help or support, then resenting the partner for not supporting them.

Workaholism as a way of avoiding intimacy. (So is boozing ...)

Pre-emptively leaving relationships out of fear of rejection, or having serial relationships ("conquests") as a way of bolstering their self-image.

Haranguing the partner for not reflecting well on them, for behaving in ways that do not support the Three's self-image.

Type Compatibility

To learn more about compatibility issues and relationships with other types, see the Enneagram Type Combinations.

The Passion: Deceit (Vanity)

Deceit here is primarily a kind of self-deception. Threes convince themselves that only their image and their performance are valuable. They subconsciously feel that their own natural inner qualities are inadequate or unacceptable, so they strive to become the sort of person that they believe others would look up to. They have an idea of the qualities, talents, and appearance that they need to have in order to be acceptable, and they work tirelessly to embody those qualities.

Thus, Threes convince themselves that they must always be outstanding, superb, and exceptional—the best at whatever they are focusing on. To be any less than this is to fail, to be worthless. This is like the child who gets straight A's but is then tormented by getting an A-minus or a B-plus, or the athlete who wins several gold medals but then feels like a failure for getting a silver or bronze. This kind of self-rejection and self-deception causes Threes a great deal of suffering. Once Threes lose themselves in these self-deceptions, truth becomes whatever works to keep their self-image going, and they are able to deceive others, often without any apparent remorse.

At Their Best

Healthy Threes are excellent communicators, motivators, and promoters, and they know how to present something in a way that's acceptable and attractive. In the workplace, they can be very effective at building morale and company spirit. They value excellence and accomplishment and truly enjoy helping others discover how to shine. Even when they are not "coaching" others, they often inspire people to become like them in some way.

Healthy Threes are able to do this because they believe in themselves and invest time and energy in developing their native talents. They value themselves, their lives, and the people they love, seeing life as an opportunity to offer what talents they have been given to the world. They are also "adaptable" in the best sense of the word. If they see that they are doing something incorrectly or that their methods are not reaping positive results, they are willing to learn another way and to change. Further, healthy Threes are not in a contest with anyone. They deeply enjoy working with others toward shared goals and do not need to outshine their peers.

Thus, healthy Threes may or may not have significant accomplishments, but others are impressed by their realness and their heartfelt sincerity. They model an honesty, simplicity, and authenticity that inspires people. They do not try to impress others or inflate their importance; rather, they see their limitations and appreciate their talents without taking themselves too seriously. At their best, they are also tender, touchingly genuine, and affectionate—they truly become "heroes" and "role models" who inspire others by their outstanding achievements, humility, and warmth.

Personality Dynamics & Variations

Learn more about the Directions of Integration (Security) and Disintegration (Stress).

Under Stress (Three Goes to Average Nine)

When Threes drive themselves too hard, their stress can go beyond what they can normally cope with. When this occurs, they tend to go on "autopilot," attempting to just get through things without being bothered, in the manner of average Nines. Threes going to Nine become more passive and fall into routines. They lose their focus and involve themselves with busywork to at least give the appearance that they are getting things done. If stress continues, however, they may begin to become shut down, listless, and depressed, losing interest in their projects and withdrawing from people. They feel little energy or enthusiasm and simply want people to leave them alone and give them space.

They can become stubborn and resistant to offers of help at these times, not wanting to hear that they have a problem.

Security (Three Goes to Average Six)

With most people, Threes make every effort to be diplomatic and well-mannered. They do not want to say things that would be off-putting to people if they can avoid it. But when Threes feel that their relationships are secure, they can be more open about expressing their anxieties and frustrations. They may keep a "positive frame of mind" all day at work, only to come home and download their dissatisfaction onto their spouse or partner. ("I think my boss is going to go nuts on me when he finds out we still haven't got this report nailed down.") Feelings of self-doubt, dread, suspicion, and anger at others' incompetence can all surface in contrast to the Three's usual "can do" attitude.

Integration (Three Goes to Healthy Six)

As Threes let go of their fears of failure and worthlessness, they start to feel less competitive with others. They relax and find that they feel most valuable while working cooperatively with others toward shared goals and aspirations, like healthy Sixes. They learn to freely offer support and guidance to the people in their lives, but more importantly, they also learn to ask for support when they need it. Threes ordinarily put themselves under such pressure to accomplish their goals with little or no help that it comes as both a surprise and a relief to them that others are happy to help them in their endeavors. In short, Threes learn to trust others and to build lasting bonds with people.

They become more selfless and courageous, embodying real qualities of leadership and self-sacrifice. By letting go of their need to outshine others, Threes become truly extraordinary human beings.

The Levels of Development

Learn more about the nine Levels of Development.

Healthy Levels

Level 1 (At Their Best): Self-accepting, inner-directed, and authentic, everything they seem to be. Modest and charitable, self-deprecatory humor and a fullness of heart emerge. Gentle and benevolent.

Level 2: Self-assured, energetic, and competent with high self-esteem: they believe in themselves and their own value. Adaptable, desirable, charming, and gracious.

Level 3: Ambitious to improve themselves, to be "the best they can be"—often become outstanding, a human ideal, embodying widely admired cultural qualities. Highly effective: others are motivated to be like them in some positive way.

Average Levels

Level 4: Highly concerned with their performance, doing their job well, constantly driving self to achieve goals as if self-worth depends on it. Terrified of failure. Compare self with others in search for status and success. Become careerists, social climbers, invested in exclusivity and being the "best."

Level 5: Become image-conscious, highly concerned with how they are perceived. Begin to package themselves according to the expectations of others and what they need to do to be successful. Pragmatic and efficient, but also premeditated, losing touch with their own feelings beneath a smooth facade. Problems with intimacy, credibility, and "phoniness" emerge.

Level 6: Want to impress others with their superiority: constantly promoting themselves, making themselves sound better than they really are. Narcissistic, with grandiose, inflated notions about themselves and their talents. Exhibitionistic and seductive, as if saying "Look at me!" Arrogance and contempt for others is a defense against feeling jealous of others and their success.

Unhealthy Levels

Level 7: Fearing failure and humiliation, they can be exploitative and opportunistic, covetous of the success of others, and willing to do "whatever it takes" to preserve the illusion of their superiority.

Level 8: Devious and deceptive so that their mistakes and wrongdoings will not be exposed. Untrustworthy, maliciously betraying or sabotaging people to triumph over them. Delusionally jealous of others

Level 9: Become vindictive, attempting to ruin others' happiness. Relentless, obsessive about destroying whatever reminds them of their own shortcomings and failures. Psychopathic behavior. Generally corresponds to the Narcissistic Personality Disorder.

Personal Growth Recommendations for Type Threes

Threes grow by recognizing that they do not need to separate their work and functioning from their feelings. Threes believe they will be less effective and competent if they allow their feelings to enter the picture. Thus, they wait until they are done with theirtasks before they pay any attention to their emotions. Nonetheless, their emotions are always operating, even if unconsciously. And if Threes neglect them too long, those emotions start to make functioning much more difficult. Thus, growth for Threes entails pausing while working and actively checking in with their feelings. By tuning in to their heart, and becoming more conscious of their inner life, Threes derive much greater happiness and satisfaction from their work and from their relationships.

For our real development, it is essential to be truthful. Be honest with yourself and others about your genuine feelings and needs. Likewise, resist the temptation to impress others or inflate your importance. You will impress people more deeply by being authentic than by bragging about your successes or exaggerating your accomplishments.

Develop charity and cooperation in your relationships. You can do this by taking time to pause in busy day to really connect with someone you care about. Nothing spectacular is required—simply a few moments of quiet appreciation. When you do so, you will become a more loving person, a more faithful friend—and a much more desirable individual. You will feel better about yourself.

Take breaks. You can drive yourself and others to exhaustion with your relentless pursuit of your goals. Ambition and self-development are good qualities, but temper them with rest periods in which you reconnect more deeply with yourself.

Sometimes taking three to five deep breaths is enough to recharge your battery and improve your outlook.

Develop your social awareness. Many Threes have grown tremendously by getting involved in projects that had nothing to do with their own personal advancement.

Working cooperatively with others toward goals that transcend personal interest is a powerful way of finding your true value and identity.

In their desire to be accepted by others, some average Threes adapt so much to the expectations of others that they lose touch with what they are really feeling about the situation. Develop yourself by resisting doing what is acceptable just to be accepted. It is imperative that you invest time in discovering your own core values.

Examples

Augustus Caesar, Emperor Constantine, Bill Clinton, Tony Blair, Prince William, Condoleeza Rice, Arnold Schwarzenegger,

Carl Lewis, Muhammed Ali, John Edwards, Mitt Romney, Bill Wilson (AA Founder), Andy Warhol, Truman Capote, Werner Erhard, Oprah Winfrey, Deepak Chopra, Tony Robbins, Bernie Madoff, Bryant Gumbel, Michael Jordan, O.J. Simpson, Tiger Woods, Lance Armstrong, Elvis Presley, Paul McCartney, Madonna, Sting, Whitney Houston, Jon Bon Jovi, Lady Gaga, Taylor Swift, Justin Bieber, Brooke Shields, Cindy Crawford, Tom Cruise, Barbra Streisand, Ben Kingsley, Jamie Foxx, Richard Gere, Ken Watanake, Will Smith, Courteney Cox, Demi Moore, Kevin Spacey, Reese Witherspoon, Anne Hathaway, Chef Daniel Boulud, Dick Clark, Ryan Seacrest, Cat Deeley, Mad Men's "Don Draper," Glee's "Rachel Berry".

Personality Type SEVEN: The Enthusiast

The Busy, Variety-Seeking Type:

Spontaneous, Versatile, Distractible, and Scattered

Generally, Sevens are excitable, spontaneous, curious, optimistic, eager, outgoing, future-oriented, adventurous, variety seeking, quick, and talkative.

Sevens get into conflicts by being scattered, distracted, restless, impatient, thrill-seeking, escapist, over-extended, irresponsible, demanding, and excessive.

At their best, Sevens are appreciative, bountiful, thoughtful, accomplished, versatile, receptive, grateful, content, quiet, and passionate.

Recognizing Sevens

Type Seven exemplifies the desire for freedom and variety and for exploring the many rich experiences that life offers. Thus, Sevens are probably the most enthusiastic, extroverted, and outgoing type of the Enneagram. They are spontaneous and upbeat; they find life exhilarating. They are the kind of people who make ordinary life into a celebration. Sevens like to fill up their calendar with things to do: after work, a quick drink; then off to dinner and the theater; then after that, a nightcap before getting home at 2 a.m. The next night may bring the symphony, a ball game, or singing in the local choir, or a visit to new restaurant. Sevens who do not live in large cities or who do not have enough money for that diverse a lifestyle might have to make do with less lavishness. But they still seek variety and constant experience, whether it's going to a mall or out to a movie, talking on the phone with friends, hanging out in a bar, or leafing through magazines and daydreaming about a vacation. Sevens do their best to stay up with what's new, and so their wide-ranging experience makes them a resource for others, too.

They know which Italian restaurant, or cognac, or jeweler is the best; they know what new movies are worth seeing and what the latest news and trends are.

Healthy Sevens, however, know that life is most satisfying when they keep their feet on the ground and work within certain constraints. Their enthusiasm and versatility can make them productive and practical, highly creative and prolific, cross-fertilizing their many areas of interest and skills. They can be highly accomplished "Renaissance people," gifted with virtuosic talents and prodigious skills. If they suffer a setback or disappointment, Sevens bounce back with resilience and renewed energy: very little keeps them down for long.

Sevens want to try everything at least twice: once to see what it is like, and the second time to see if they liked it the first time! Of course, Sevens want their experiences to be as much fun and as enjoyable as possible, although, strictly speaking, that is not always essential. What is important to Sevens is being free, having options, and creating more possibilities for their future.

Sevens' minds are restless and filled with ideas and plans for activities to look forward to.

They anticipate the future, virtually licking their lips as they foresee the delicious possibilities that await them. But Sevens do not just think about the future: they get out there and actually make it happen. They live their dreams by throwing themselves into action and putting their plans in motion. With their energy and enthusiasm, they get things going!

However, as their restlessness increases and they begin to fear missing out on other pleasures and experiences, average Sevens become less discriminate about the experiences they pursue. They begin to lose a sense of priorities and become hyperactive, throwing themselves into constant activity—into endless busyness. They easily feel trapped or deprived, and this makes it difficult to say "no" to themselves or to deny themselves anything. While this might seem like freedom to them, it is a kind of prison that makes it increasingly difficult for them to find satisfaction in what they are doing. They begin to believe that freedom is having no restrictions or responsibilities, but this is a false freedom, and it eventually brings them greater unhappiness.

As this occurs, Sevens begin to flee from their inner anxieties by engaging in more distractions and activities. They expect that they and their lives should be exciting and "dazzling" all the time. Increasingly uninhibited, they grab attention and discharge anxiety with storytelling, joking around, exaggeration, and wise-cracking. Others may find this behavior amusing and irreverently entertaining for a while, but for most people, even other Sevens, scattered energy eventually becomes tiresome. This only frustrates average Sevens, and unless others are willing to keep up with them, for better or worse, the Seven moves on to greener pastures. Often, this leads to a dissipation of their energy and a loss of focus. While Sevens are often brilliant, once in flight from themselves, they often fail to actualize their many talents or live up to their potential.

In brief, Sevens want to maintain their freedom and happiness, to have a wide variety of interesting, fun experiences and choices, to keep their options open, to avoid missing out on anything worthwhile, to have more pleasure, to keep themselves excited and occupied, and to avoid and discharge pain. Sevens do not want to feel trapped or limited by having few choices or options, to be bored or guilty, to let their anxieties arise for long, to be slowed down, to be still and quiet for long periods of time, or to dwell in the past.

Their Hidden Side

On the surface, Sevens would like to convince themselves and everyone else that they are always feeling "fabulous"— having the time of their lives. Of course, the truth is often somewhat different. Sevens, like all human beings, are vulnerable to anxiety, depression, loneliness, and other difficult feelings. At times, Sevens sincerely want to tell others how they actually feel, but they often feel compelled to keep spirits high, even if privately they are miserable themselves. Yet they also struggle with fears of not being taken seriously and a sense that others will misinterpret their positive approach to life as a lack of feeling or depth. In private, Sevens struggle with loneliness, grief, and self-doubt and are as prone to depression as any other type.

Most of all, Sevens fear a gnawing feeling that they will never really get what they truly want in life. So they settle for other pleasures that they hope will make them happy enough, or at least pleasantly distracted, from the more painful disappointments in their lives.

Relationship Issues

Sevens are often sought out as companions because of their energy, openness to experience, and high spirits. They are like a breath of fresh air to more withdrawn or subdued types and can generally be relied on to be stimulating, engaging, and fun.

Sevens can also be generous with themselves and their resources. They feel that good times are best enjoyed when others are enjoying them too and they want to have someone to share their adventures and discoveries with. But the very high-energy approach that draws people to Sevens can also exhaust their partners. Others can tire of the nonstop stream of activities and plans and want more quiet time with Sevens, which less healthy Sevens may resist. Other relationship problems include these:

Becoming so involved with expressing their thoughts and ideas that they do not really listen to others.

Becoming impatient or critical of others' slower pace.

Getting flighty or seeking distractions when important relationship challenges arise.

Fearing that others will not support them if they are down or depressed.

Expecting the partner to provide gratification, entertainment, or support immediately on demand.

Being unwilling—or very slow—to make commitments.

Type Compatibility

To learn more about compatibility issues and relationships with other types, see the Enneagram Type Combinations.

The Passion: Gluttony

Sevens enjoy life most when they feel stimulated, awake, and refreshed by life's amazing diversity. But to the extent that they are harboring unacknowledged feelings of inner emptiness or loneliness, Sevens become anxious and can get into the habit of seeking constant stimulation as a way of distracting themselves from their anxiety. At such times, they are like starving refugees released at a banquet: they gobble up every experience that is offered to them, often without discriminating the experiences that would be most satisfying. And because their minds are so revved up with options and exciting possibilities, the experiences that they are having hold little possibility for actually getting through to them. Sevens are so much looking forward to the next great experience that the experience they are having now cannot satisfy them. Thus, they remain in a state of perpetual hunger—restlessly seeking the magic combination of circumstances that they believe will fulfil them once and for all.

At Their Best

When they are balanced and in their own center, healthy Sevens can harness their enormous enthusiasm and curiosity and still stay focused and deeply engaged with tasks until they are brought to completion. They can set priorities and work within limitations, imposing restrictions on themselves from the recognition that a certain degree of self-restraint actually makes them more productive and much happier. Healthy Sevens can say "no:" to themselves without feeling deprived because they are more in touch with their own Inner Guidance and their ability to know what will fulfill them most deeply. From this sense of fulfillment, healthy Sevens move toward others and to the world from a sense of abundance and joy, feeling intensely blessed to be alive and able to enjoy the many enriching experiences that life brings them.

Healthy Sevens are also steady and grounded, able to honor commitments and to take personal responsibility for their actions. In short, they grow up emotionally and move from being an "eternal youth" to being a mature person, able to look both inward at themselves and outward at life, accepting all that they find in both realms. They become truly "celebratory" and filled with gratitude, resolving their inner hunger and allowing them to feel that they never have to fear that they will be deprived of anything truly worthwhile.

Personality Dynamics & Variations

Learn more about the Directions of Integration (Security) and Disintegration (Stress).

Under Stress (Seven Goes to Average One)

Sevens value their spontaneity and so tend to follow their impulses, for better or for worse. As a result, they can become scattered in their attention and energy, leaping from one promising idea to the next, from one activity to another. While this can be exciting, it often leaves Sevens frustrated with themselves because they feel that they are not accomplishing as much as they would like to. At such times, they begin to behave like average Ones— pulling in the reins on themselves and trying to get more organized and self-controlled. But because they are trying to impose order and control on themselves, they begin to feel trapped and restricted. This only makes them more frustrated, impatient, and irritable. They may, for instance, become critical of their own creative ideas before they have really had a chance to develop them. Similarly, they cannot avoid feeling disappointment with people and many aspects of their environment. Nothing seems to meet their expectations, and they can become harsh and perfectionistically critical with themselves and with others.

Security (Seven Goes to Average Five)

Sevens often feel it is their duty to entertain others and to keep their environment positive and exciting. Over time, this can be exhausting—even for Sevens. When they are tired of being "on" for everyone, they may choose to withdraw even from their intimates and seek seclusion and noninterference. This can come as a shock to others. ("You've been out having fun with everyone else, so why are you so quiet and unavailable with me?") They no longer want to put out energy for anyone else, and can become almost obsessively focused and preoccupied. They can also be surprisingly withdrawn and isolated, like Fives. Their body language and aloof responses let others know that they want space and privacy. At such times, Sevens make no effort to entertain or energize others. Like Fives, they retreat from contact and attempt to restore their energy.

Integration (Seven Goes to Healthy Five)

As Sevens learn to relax and to tolerate their uncomfortable feelings more completely, they stop using their restless minds to distract themselves. Their minds become quiet, clear, and focused, allowing Sevens to tap more deeply into their reserves of creativity and insight. They are able to prioritize not by imposing some arbitrary order on themselves but by following their true interests and staying with them. Thus, they become far more productive, satisfied, and really satisfying as companions. Their capacity to find connections and to synthesize information is not drawn off into tangents—they produce results, and this gives them grounds for real confidence in themselves and in life. As they experience the world more deeply, they find each moment fascinating, profound, and revelatory. The idea of boredom becomes absurd as they savor the incredible mysteries of existence, moment by moment.

The Levels of Development

Learn more about the nine Levels of Development.

Healthy Levels

Level 1 (At Their Best): Assimilate experiences in depth, making them deeply grateful and appreciative for what they have. Become awed by the simple wonders of life: joyous and ecstatic. Intimations of spiritual reality, of the boundless goodness of life.

Level 2: Highly responsive, excitable, enthusiastic about sensation and experience. Most extroverted type: stimuli bring immediate responses—they find everything invigorating. Lively, vivacious, eager, spontaneous, resilient, cheerful.

Level 3: Easily become accomplished achievers, generalists who do many different things well: multi-talented. Practical, productive, usually prolific, cross-fertilizing areas of interest.

Average Levels

Level 4: As restlessness increases, want to have more options and choices available to them. Become adventurous and "worldly wise," but less focused, constantly seeking new things and experiences: the sophisticate, connoisseur, and consumer. Money, variety, keeping up with the latest trends important.

Level 5: Unable to discriminate what they really need, become hyperactive, unable to say "no" to themselves, throwing self into constant activity. Uninhibited, doing and saying whatever comes to mind: storytelling, flamboyant exaggerations, witty wise-cracking, performing. Fear being bored: in perpetual motion, but do too many things—many ideas but little follow through.

Level 6: Get into conspicuous consumption and all forms of excess. Self-centered, materialistic, and greedy, never feeling that they have enough. Demanding and pushy, yet unsatisfied and jaded. Addictive, hardened, and insensitive.

Unhealthy Levels

Level 7: Desperate to quell their anxieties, can be impulsive and infantile: do not know when to stop. Addictions and excess take their toll: debauched, depraved, dissipated escapists, offensive and abusive.

Level 8: In flight from self, acting out impulses rather than dealing with anxiety or frustrations: go out of control, into erratic mood swings, and compulsive actions (manias).

Level 9: Finally, their energy and health is completely spent: become claustrophobic and panic-stricken. Often give up on themselves and life: deep depression and despair, self-destructive overdoses, impulsive suicide. Generally corresponds to the Bipolar disorder and Histrionic personality disorder.

Personal Growth Recommendations for Type Sevens

Sevens grow by recognizing that real happiness is available anytime, anywhere: the price of admission is their willingness and ability to be quiet, to be still inside themselves, and to open their eyes to the wonder and richness of life all around them. Once Sevens understand this, they are able to assimilate their experiences in depth. They discover that every moment can make them feel deeply grateful and appreciative—truly awed by the wonders of life. Moreover, their openness and inner quiet brings them a sense of life beyond the physical, a spiritual reality, that begins to shine through the material world.

The healthy Seven understands that by being still within, a quiet joy begins to pervade all of life—a deep satisfaction in existence that cannot ever be taken away.

Recognize your impulsiveness, and get in the habit of observing your impulses rather than giving in to them. This means letting most of your impulses pass and becoming a better judge of which ones are worth acting on. The more you can resist acting out your impulses, the more you will be able to focus on what is really good for you.

Learn to listen to other people. They are often interesting, and you may learn things that will open new doors for you. Also learn to appreciate silence and solitude: you do not have to distract yourself (and protect yourself from anxiety) with constant noise from the television or the stereo. By learning to live with less external stimulation, you will learn to trust yourself. You will be happier than you expect because you will be satisfied with whatever you do, even if it is less than you have been doing.

You do not have to have everything this very moment. That tempting new acquisition will most likely still be available tomorrow (this is certainly true of food, alcohol, and other common gratifications—that ice cream cone, for instance). Most good opportunities will come back again—and you will be in a better position to discern which opportunities really are best for you.

Always choose quality over quantity, especially in your experiences. The ability to have experiences of quality can be learned only by giving your full attention to the experience you are having now. If you keep anticipating future experiences, you will keep missing the present one and undermine the possibility of ever being satisfied.

Make sure that what you want will really be good for you in the long run. As the saying goes, watch what you pray for since your prayers may be answered. In the same vein, think about the long-term consequences of what you want since you may get it only to find that it becomes another disappointment—or even a source of unhappiness."

....

It is good to know about self ... From my recent experience, however, also knowing about the magic 'eight-second glance' per resume among modern-day recruiters, the above document has not been popular in my job-hunting submissions ... Not surprising; what a boring and long read, even for the test taker, let alone some office junior charged with the task of sifting through hundreds of applications.

I guess I am not out of line ... Mostly. But I am still rather lost, without a clear pitch, four decades into it.

During my recent tertiary IT studies at a university in New Zealand, I was introduced to the terms 'Digital Immigrants' and 'Digital Natives' ... I wrote a paper on it. The summary read like this:

> There is a commonly espoused view in technology circles, that executives can be classified as either **Digital Natives** or **Digital Immigrants** – the former being those who grew up using technologies such as the Internet and smartphones, while the latter are older and did not grow up with these tools.

> The hypothesis is that chief officers who are Digital Natives are more comfortable setting technology-related strategies and managing their implementation – even where the executive's primary competency is not IT (e.g. their background is marketing or finance).

> Therefore, as the **younger Digital Natives** mature and transition into leadership roles

in their organisations, the IT maturity of these organisations will increase and the requirement for IT-specific specialist resources may diminish.

(I must acknowledge here that this 2014 subject proposal was by Mary-Lou Hoskins, General Manager, DesignerTech.Ltd., who was to be my project sponsor. Unfortunately, due to circumstances beyond our control, the project was canned.)

In this project, recommendations were to be made regarding the familiarity and competency with information technology that can be expected from the new generation of IT leaders, so that any necessary changes to any professional practice in advising, training and mentoring these people can be incorporated.

The goal was to examine the current status-quo and to deliver a model, and predictions, with imminent outcomes on the qualities of the

Digital Immigrants transitioning to Digital Natives, as IT business-leaders, with its implications on SMEs, as well as IT-resource support companies, in light of the prevailing global trends. To critically examine, evaluate, derive, predict, anticipate, decide and recognise the issues on the topic, as well as to isolate, sample data and create a model, facilitating and predicting outcomes.

The objectives were defined, as follows:

- to provide a current 'picture' of the IT-background of the SME business leadership and how/why it is changing;

- to examine the transition of the Digital Immigrants to Digital Natives, their progression into leadership, with its implications on IT resource-support companies;

- to deliver a prognosis of what changes (if any) are required by the IT resource/support companies, sighting the technology-savvy new business leaders arriving on the arena;

- to determine the requirements and the outcomes of prevailing trends in IT business leadership;

- to supply a clear vision of what is in store, globally, for the IT industry, when business-executives are tertiary-trained experts in the field;

- to create a model, based on data-sampling, predicting an outcome.

In the ever-changing world of business and technology, it is wise to monitor any prevailing trends affecting the outcomes and of how business is conducted. It is prudent to implement changes that are required to maintain the flow, keep up with the trends and to remain strong in a competitive environment. As the global population grows, and is increasingly educated and maturing, the workforce is changing, which alters the requirements in the provision of IT specialist support.

With the above in mind, the attempt was to deliver a model and how to embrace the inevitable changes, the way IT companies support the Digital Native lead organisations.

It is worth noting that there is already literature on the subject, with expert/professional authors examining and clearly recognising this to be a topic worth our consideration. For example, Dr John Palfrey and Urs Gasser, in *Born Digital – Understanding the First Generation of Digital Natives* (2008), *Measuring the Information Society* (2013) by the International Telecommunications Union, 'Digital Natives and Digital Immigrants – Cohabitants of Digital World' (2013) by Grace Gomez, and Marc Prensky in 'The Emerging Online Life of a Digital Native' (2006), to mention a few …

Most, if not all of the questions are relevant and resonate today, perhaps even more so:

- What characteristics define whether the Digital Native will have the necessary competencies to achieve strong leadership in the IT space?

- Could the transition to an era of Digital Native leadership see a reduction in a focus on 'cool technology' – technology for its own sake rather than utilising technology to support business outcomes?

- What would the implications of that be for business, the organisation and the evolution of technology as a business tool? Or, has technology made this group more people and outcomes focused than we might be expecting – in which case, what would the implications be?

....

[Ref: Lake Argyle, Western Australia. From the Big Loop Ride Australia, July'2018]

We all love holidays, right ...? Have you ever considered a vacation in Australia ...?

As a seasoned globetrotter myself, and a professional planner/detail-fixer, I am offering to add value, with personalised, local services when you say 'yes' to a vacation in Australia. Whatever your ethnicity, language or needs. Catering for all, with a welcoming, interdenominational, multicultural sensitivity and global experience of world travel. If English is not your forte, I am comfortable with 'hand-language' (my Polish, Russian and German have all gone rusty).

Based in Brisbane, Queensland, I would love to show you and your party around, to arrange bookings for anything you require and desire, including guiding/driving, from before you arrive here, to after you depart. Your choice of luxury and budget. Please reach out with your requirements for more information and a quote at tom.zed@outlook.com. I am here to help you to enjoy a fabulous stay in Australia, with the safety, privacy and anonymity you deserve. Discretion assured!

VIII.   'QUO VADIS, DOMINE?'

Nowhere to go from here …

My survival technique, over the years, especially mentally, has been daily **gratitude** and an uptake of **endorphins**, derived by regular, vigorous exercise. Of course, without my family, in this and in my 'previous life', I would not have been able to manage any of it on my own! The transition in-between, straight after my separation/divorce, when I was on my own, lasted four years. This was both a healing time and drunken/stoned time of madness and mental disturbance and total instability – out of control. Typically, especially for a Pole, my heavy drinking became diabolical! Interestingly, I always remained physically fit though, either by regular running, as well as weightlifting ... and I was never committed for drink-driving. After Outward Bound I stepped up the healthy lifestyle, gave up the drugs (well ... the bottle's always my 'dark-friend'... I am Polish, after all!).

My wife, my youngest son and my grown-up children (externally), have given me tremendous support; particularly through the time of my difficult exit from the port job, five years of full-time studies and, most recently, two/three years of job hunting. This is all relevant to the topic of MIGRATION, since I have no doubt in my mind, that it would be very different on one's own turf, back in the motherland, with the help of one's parents and extended family. Local contacts! 'It's WHO you know, not what you know' carries a lot of truth.

Besides my periods of going 'dry', like currently, now, I continue to 'medicate' with alcohol, in a civilised, controlled/moderated manner, for reasons I cannot explain. I wonder, myself, if it's to do with feeling displaced, although I do not miss anything about Poland, or Europe! For every time I travelled back there from my base in New Zealand and Australia, I was a stranger there, a tourist, with a funny accent, even in my old hometown, worlds apart from the old mates, no longer getting the local jokes, their culture, or politics. And every time I was there, I was homesick and kissed the ground landing back in Auckland, Perth and Brisbane, on home turf. As weird as it may sound, as a migrant – you are damned if you do and damned if you don't, long term, if not forever!

I am not alone in this. Most expat/resettlers abroad whom I have met, seem to remain 'out of place'. I have known people from peaceful European countries, who decided to go and live Down Under, and they remain the ones who criticise, dislike the locals, watch European TV channels, and stick to themselves socially; and then there are those like the Afghani restaurant owner I know in Australia, who became an Australian citizen many years ago, after spending years in refugee camps overseas, who now travels back to Kabul, regularly, highly recommending for me to go there for a holiday – I don't think so, even if you paid me! These extreme cases also exist for those families who left Britain for the warm weather in Perth, then whinged about the extreme heat over there, returned back to England, returned back to Australia after a while and did it all again no less than THREE times; relocating all their possessions, selling/buying homes, changing their children's schools, their jobs and all that goes with it! WTF?! What a waste! Human nature, I guess …

Anyway … Daily, conscious gratitude is the key, no matter where you are! For we all have something to appreciate and be thankful for!

Hindsight? Would I do it again? It is not a fair question; it is actually unfair! If I remained, I would not have had my seven children I love more than anything in my life, and I most certainly would not have learned what I have in my globetrotting experiences I mentioned in this book.

I am certain my old schoolmates from Poland envy me for where I live (little do they know about what I do, or what I don't do ...), as most Europeans, Scandinavians, Americans (North and South), Asians, Africans and all others (?) dream about life on the sunny shores of Australia or New Zealand!

I know it is pointless, but also very tempting to explore the 'what ifs' ... Hypothetically thinking/speaking, I would have inherited a large family home by the forest, with a business manufacturing automotive spare parts, employing several production machine operators. I would have thrived in the local environment, compatible with my heritage, upbringing, and business and social environments. And like other prosperous Poles, I would have travelled around Europe (at least) for annual holidays, enjoyed fine automobiles, dining, theatres, movies, shopping, etc. No war, no more crime than anywhere else in the developed world … This poses my favorite, although rhetorical question: WTF? … well, I don't know!

As I now reminisce on the past and how I am, today, personally and socially among the locals Down Under (it could be anywhere else, for that matter …), I continue to feel like I am a misfit, most of the time. And it is not to say that I don't have the skills or the eloquence to interact! On the contrary, I can do the small talk, chit-chat – if/when I have to. However, I do despise the shallow jokes, the forced laughter and the macho-man/sports/loud blabber … There are at least three reasons for this. One: I have an introvert type personality (which is not entirely true). Two: I have been conditioned and brought up to be 'the best' (whatever that means …), better than others, which has really disturbed my real self-value. Or three: my (Polish) background makes me unfit, unsuitable to blend into any society outside the motherland ... Remember, it has been forty years since I left, so what does this make me ...? A rhetorical question, remaining unanswered, quite hurtful and maybe 'open' forever ...

I now have a loving family, right where I am, in a clean, safe space, where the weather is always fine and life is generally good! Apparently, I am free to do what I choose. Democracy provides me with a vote for a government I deem most suitable, in line with my beliefs ... Why and what could I possibly wish for, realistically ...!

Perhaps the whole of my oratory on migration here is bullshit and that it is me, personally, who is so fucked up for various reasons, that prevents me from becoming a 'true-blue' local ... Not by observing and judging so many others I've met! Maybe there is a 'gypsy' in us all ... Maybe the grass is greener on the other side ... The price you pay to check it out is far greater than the airfares! You can trust me on that! For every postcard is designed to look pretty … but 'you can't eat the scenery'.

'Give me four years to teach the children and the seed I have sown will never be uprooted.' Vladimir Lenin.

There is another take on how we assimilate to a different environment, based on the old adage that 'Home is where you lay your head'… and where your beloved (family, friends, pets, etc.) are.

'The Gift of a Bicultural Upbringing' by Sandhya Fuchs, 10/Jan.2020 published on Sapiens. Sapiens.org

"A daughter of anthropologists reflects on how a childhood lived in and between two cultures profoundly shapes one's views of belonging and "othering."

Sandhya Fuchs is a Leverhulme Trust Ph.D. scholar in anthropology at the London School of Economics and Political Science.

I remember distinctly the moment I realized I had two childhoods. I was in third grade and had waddled down the hill of my suburban German neighborhood to wait for the bus. My best friend was waiting there with her mother, and an exasperated group of parents was discussing the head lice epidemic plaguing our school. When I arrived, my friend's mother turned around to scrutinize me.

"Let me see your head!" she demanded. "You have spent so much time in India, and people over there are very unhygienic, so *you* probably brought in the lice!" Then she added: "It's just very different over there. They don't have the same standards. Your parents really shouldn't take you to such a place!"

As she examined my scalp, I gulped in a failed attempt to swallow rising tears. I didn't know why, but I felt sad, slightly ashamed, and out of place. Later that day when I relayed the story to my father, he was furious. While he raged about prejudice and racism—big words I didn't fully understand—I thought about my double life.

Every year between the ages of 5 and 13, I went with my parents—both trained anthropologists and scholars of South Asia—to the Himalayas, where my mother conducted in-depth fieldwork. I learned Hindi, and the family we stayed with became our family.

Half the year I went to school in Germany, took flute lessons, and competed on the swim team. The other half, I learned about Himalayan agriculture, watched water buffalo and goats wander through our village, and excitedly awaited the newest Bollywood films. I loved both places. Both were home. And even though the settings couldn't have been more different, I never truly drew a line between Germany and India in my mind.

But after the lice incident, I wondered: *Was there something wrong with my village life? Was it weird? Were my friends there so different from my friends here?* It began to dawn on me that my life had two different parts. And I thought, *if I want to truly belong to one, would I have to give up the other?*

Over the years, as I've seen the world increasingly divided by notions of "us versus them" and have set out on my anthropological studies of caste issues in India, I have reflected on these issues frequently.

Most people are taught from a young age to make distinctions between themselves and "others" or "here and there." But the children of anthropologists—much like other children raised in a cross-cultural environment—frequently struggle to make those distinctions. Their upbringing profoundly shapes the ways they interact with people from various cultures and places who hold vastly different viewpoints.

So, I believe the lessons from an anthropological childhood are particularly important today as "us versus them" debates dominate sociopolitical conversations. These lessons can help people answer powerful questions about belonging, "othering," and connecting: Does truly belonging in one group mean we must "other" people who are outside that sphere? Is universal empathy only possible by living as an outsider? And most important of all, how can we connect with people whose lives and perspectives seem so different from ours?

In the 1990s, when my mother conducted fieldwork, she was never without her camera. She owned a slightly battered vintage Kodak Six that she loved fiercely. Watching her from the backseat of a car, or from the squeaky wooden balcony of the room we rented in a joint family home in what is now the Indian state of Uttarakhand, I used to think research consisted mainly of photographing the world and people around us.

The route to a new sense of familiarity and belonging tends to follow the same bends in the road.

The images of my mother climbing on rooftops, wading through dense crowds, or stopping the car without warning to get that one good shot have haunted me. They haunt me because unlike her, I was never so keen or comfortable taking that shot—a photograph that essentially marks its creator as an outsider. And I always felt a little uneasy admitting I was an outsider.

Even though I understood on some level that we were moving between countries, I did not conceive of Germany and India as separate experiences. They were just different seasons with different friends, and I always enjoyed telling one about the other. Happily unconcerned with disparities between nations or communities, I simply looked forward to the different moments of my life spent entertaining people (and sometimes goats) anywhere.

"I think we intuitively learn to fit in," says a friend whose anthropologist mother also dragged her around the world. "I don't mean in a follow-the-peer-pressure kind of way. I mean in the sense that you kind of always know what it means to make community and be part of it. And you realize that the process is the same wherever you go."

Her statement points to an important insight: As much as we learn something novel when moving to a new cultural setting—how to prepare a meal, greet someone, or tell an appropriate joke—the route to a new sense of familiarity and belonging tends to follow the same bends in the road.

As different as cultures are on some levels, the process of open engagement and interaction that forms the heart of home and belonging is probably similar everywhere. In this process, different ideas of family life or what registers as funny bleed into one another. Without needing to be compared, demarcated, or analyzed, these habits simply coexist—sometimes separately, sometimes in conversation with one another.

At the same time, intuitively learning to fit in everywhere comes at a cost.

When my mother did fieldwork, her tendency to jump around with her enormous camera or travel without a male companion—even though other women in the village would not—was accepted. If her behavior inspired some gossip, she was still entitled to her eccentricities as a "Western woman."

But for me, expectations seemed different, both when I was growing up in Uttarakhand and when I later conducted fieldwork in Rajasthan, India. The transgressions my mother was allowed were, while possible, certainly more discouraged for me—someone who spoke Hindi fluently and had adopted particular cultural mannerisms and local forms of humor from a young age.

"Sandhya may look Western, but she is one of our girls," the mother of my host family in Rajasthan used to tell people. "She doesn't behave like most Westerners."

Even when I spent a week volunteering in a refugee camp in Swaziland (now called Eswatini), a country I didn't get to know until much later in life, the camp manager, a Swazi mother of four, used to squeeze me tight and say, "You are a good girl—just like one of ours."

Implicit in both statements was a responsibility to adhere to local codes and behavioral boundaries that outsiders—including my mother—were exempt from. Perhaps it was self-imposed, but there seemed to be a subtle contract of belonging that I had to negotiate in a different way and that demanded a level of conformity. This is the price of blending in.

Because of this, children who grow up immersed in anthropologic field experiences can simultaneously be the ultimate insider and the forever outsider. Equipped with the behavioral, psychological, and linguistic toolbox to become part of many worlds without drawing categorical boundaries between them, we exist more directly at the margins than most. Adopting a single national, professional, or personal category of identity seems suffocating.

But does that mean people can only truly belong to a group if they conform? Can those who live at the margins between groups and places still have a sense of belonging?

My partner, who was born and raised in Southern England, was heartbroken when his parents sold his childhood home when he was in his late 20s. He says it made him feel like he had lost not only a home, but an identity. His sense of belonging was spatial. Home was a place, a family, and a community at a particular point in time. He was determined to buy the house back someday in order to rebuild his fractured sense of belonging.

I empathize with him, but I can't fully comprehend his need for geographical settledness. Home for me has always been my family. Home is wherever they are.

On the other hand, unlike my partner, I have often agonized about the no man's land of my identity. I never feel more German than when I live far away from Europe. At the same time, I am most certainly not Indian or anything else. In India, I am a Westerner. To the Americans with whom I attended college in Maine, I was European. My British boyfriend thinks I am quite Continental. And in Germany, I still am that strange kid who grew up in India.

Despite all this, I believe people who lack a certain rootedness can still have a sense of belonging.

People tend to think of belonging as a binary option: You either do or you don't. In reality, most people negotiate shades of belonging in different areas of their life. Someone might acknowledge deep roots in a place they no longer live in and don't plan to return to. Someone might be raised in a certain religion yet become nonreligious.

People who are unfamiliar can nonetheless be yours.These scenarios don't imply that a person does not belong. Rather, their feelings of belonging are simply different: They can be multiple, dual or singular, liminal or complete.

Growing up inside a community, yet traversing between places and ways of belonging, can teach you countless valuable lessons: People who are unfamiliar can nonetheless be yours. The opposition between you and the "other" ultimately doesn't hold up. You have a capacity within you for growth and otherness—to become multifaceted. You can be part of many things without losing yourself. Not being completely one thing does not make you a person without a home or an identity but someone who can belong in myriad places with a variety of people.

This perspective has profound implications for today's increasingly divided world.

During my fieldwork in Rajasthan, I worked with Dalits, members of India's lowest caste who are also referred to as "untouchables." I was surprised that many of my Dalit informants, who had explicit concerns about the discrimination and exclusion they experienced daily, seemed unwilling to extend their concern to other communities.

When I told a Dalit activist that I was visiting a Muslim family in the neighborhood, she was appalled. "You should stay away from Muslims," she warned. "They treat women really badly and strategically try to have as many children as possible to become a stronger political force!"

I was stunned. As a woman who devoted her life to battling the caste-based prejudice and abuse that she deemed inhumane, how could she speak about other groups in this way?

Abstract notions of "us versus them" are at the heart of Brexit, U.S. immigration policies, and the growing influence of nationalist parties in Germany, India, and elsewhere. Discussions about distinctions cause us to wonder whether it is possible to be part of different communities on equal terms or whether truly belonging to one group means exclusion from all others.

What I've learned from an anthropological childhood is this: Having a deep feeling of being part of a community, nation, or place doesn't limit a person's capacity for empathy. But embracing a multifaceted notion of our identity prevents us from drawing potentially dangerous lines between us and other cultures, professions, countries, or political parties.

What makes a person genuinely able to embrace difference is a moment of stepping across the boundaries of one's early identity and the assumptions that accompany it. This allows for the emergence of new questions, new ideas of selfhood, and new social connections. We must be willing to face the possibility of finding ourselves out there at the margins between groups, and to welcome the discomfort of growing and learning in ways we never expected.

This growth may ultimately lead us away from the security of a comfortable, unquestioned sense of belonging. And it will make it almost impossible to declare an entire country an unhygienic place filled with strange people, the way my friend's mother described India. Because a view like that from inside a contained culture, surrounded by emotional glass walls, distorts the way we can and should think of others. That protective glass denies us the potential for connection.

Two years ago, I met up with my primary school friend, the one whose mother catapulted me into a precocious identity crisis.

"I am doing a master's in anthropology now," she told me, to my utter surprise. When I asked her about her decision, she replied: "I don't know, there was just something about hanging out with you and your parents that made me realize that faraway places or people in other cultural contexts don't have to seem far away. It made me feel like I didn't even understand what 'difference' meant and that maybe I had all these wrong ideas of other places. I looked at your family and thought, 'They are all anthropologists;

maybe if I study anthropology, I will see the world in a new way!'"

I hope she will. An anthropological life—whether it be one given to you in childhood, one you explore in a university while doing fieldwork, or simply one you adopt as an outlook—is one whose heart beats to the notion of interaction. Personal interaction has the power to counteract the dangers of abstraction. And it allows us to embrace a multiplicity of belonging in such a way that we never have to feel rootless or marginal."

[REFERENCE: Fuchs S. 'The Gift of a Bicultural Upbringing' Sapiens.org. January 2020]

Tom Zed, Queensland, Australia.

■ 2019TomZed http://www.tomzed.com.au

www.ingramcontent.com/pod-product-compliance
Lightning Source LLC
Chambersburg PA
CBHW072100020426
42334CB00017B/1578